The Forest and the Trees

ALSO BY ALLAN G. JOHNSON

NONFICTION

The Gender Knot

Privilege, Power, and Difference

The Blackwell Dictionary of Sociology

FICTION

The First Thing and the Last

Nothing Left to Lose

ALLAN G. JOHNSON

The Forest and the Trees

Sociology as Life, Practice, and Promise

THIRD EDITION

TEMPLE UNIVERSITY PRESS
PHILADELPHIA

TEMPLE UNIVERSITY PRESS
Philadelphia, Pennsylvania 19122
www.temple.edu/tempress

Copyright © 2014 by Allan G. Johnson
All rights reserved
Published 2014

Library of Congress Cataloging-in-Publication Data

Johnson, Allan G.
 The forest and the trees : sociology as life, practice, and promise / Allan G. Johnson.
— Third edition.
    pages cm
 Includes bibliographical references and index.
 ISBN 978-1-4399-1186-0 (hardback : alk. paper) — ISBN 978-1-4399-1187-7
(paper : alk. paper) — ISBN 978-1-4399-1188-4 (e-book) 1. Sociology. I. Title.
 HM585.J64 2014
 301—dc23

                                                                    2014006587

♾ The paper used in this publication meets the requirements of the American
National Standard for Information Sciences—Permanence of Paper for Printed
Library Materials, ANSI Z39.48-1992

Printed in the United States of America

9 8 7 6 5 4

For Alice

Contents

Acknowledgments   *ix*

Introduction: Life, Practice, and Promise   *1*

1 The Forest, the Trees, and the One Thing   *7*

2 Culture: Symbols, Ideas, and the Stuff of Life   *31*

3 The Structures of Social Life   *63*

4 Population and Human Ecology: People, Space, and Place   *91*

5 Us, It, and Social Interaction   *107*

6 Things Are Not What They Seem   *125*

7 Sociology as Worldview: Where White Privilege Came From   *147*

   Epilogue: Who Are We Really?   *161*

   Notes   *165*

   Glossary   *175*

   Index   *181*

Acknowledgments

For their thoughtful feedback and suggestions in the preparation of the third edition, I am grateful to Terence McGinn (University of Michigan), Elisabeth M. Lucal (Indiana University South Bend), Michael Schwalbe (North Carolina State University), and anonymous reviewers for Temple University Press. I am especially grateful to my editor, Janet Francendese, for her enthusiastic support for my work, and those whose hard work brought the book into print—production editor Joan Vidal, design director Kate Nichols, and copy editor Heather Wilcox.

Introduction

Life, Practice, and Promise

I am a practicing sociologist, and this book is about what it is that I practice, what it means, and why it matters. This book is about how the practice finds its way into almost every aspect of life, from headlines in the news to the experience of growing older to the ravages of war, injustice, oppression, and terrorism in the world. It is about things small and large, things simple and things far more complex than what we can imagine.

I practice sociology in many ways. I practice it when I think about how social life works, when I write books, and when I work with people trying to see what is going on in the world and our lives in it. I practice as a public speaker and workshop facilitator to help solve the dilemmas of a diverse and difficult world in which race, gender, sexual orientation, disability status, and other forms of privilege, power, and oppression cast dark shadows over people's lives. I practice when I read the news or turn on the television or go to the movies. I practice when I walk down a street, shop in a market, or sit in a sidewalk restaurant and watch the world go by and wonder what life *really* is all about, what this stream of interconnected people's lives consists of, what knits it all together and what tears it apart, and what it has to do with me.

I practice sociology for many reasons. I practice because there is so much unnecessary suffering in the world and because to do something about that suffering, we need to understand where it comes from. In this sense, practicing sociology has a profoundly moral dimension. I mean 'moral' not in the sense of being good instead of bad but in a deeper and broader sociological sense that touches on the essence of what we are about as human beings and what our life together consists of. It is impossible to study social life for very long without coming up against the consequences that social life produces, and many of these consequences do such damage not only to people's lives but to other species and the Earth itself, that, unless we find ways to deny or ignore reality, we feel compelled to ask, "Why?" And once we ask that question, we need tools to help make sense of where it leads and to imagine how we might go from there toward something better.

We cannot help but be part of the problem, but practicing sociology is a way to also be part of the solution. This not only helps the world but also makes it easier to live in, especially given how crazy a place it can be. It helps to be able to see how one thing is connected to another and, in that, how to find ways to make a difference, however small. We cannot change the world all by ourselves, but we can make informed decisions about how to participate in it and thereby help turn the world toward something better, even if it is in our neighborhoods or families or where we work or go to school.

I would not practice sociology if I didn't believe something better was possible. I believe that the choices we make as individuals matter beyond our lives more than we can imagine, that things don't have to be the way they are but that they will not get better all by themselves. We need to do something, and what we do needs to be based on more than hunches and personal opinion and prejudice. We need systematic ways to figure things out, and that is what sociological practice provides.

I also practice sociology because it helps me keep in touch with the essence of my own life in the world, for sociology isn't simply about some larger world 'out there.' It is also about each of us in the world and the connection between the two, which means it can take us toward basic truths about who we are and what our lives are about. I practice sociology as a way to remind myself that for all that we think we know about things, beneath that knowledge is all that we do *not* know, which is good reason to feel some awe.

There are times, for example, when I am amazed that social life works at all, that we are able to live and work together as much as we do, to talk, dream, imagine, fight, and create. There is something miraculous about the simplest conversation, in the sense that we can never get to a core truth about how it happens. We can contemplate the miracle of things by taking ourselves toward the limit of what we can know. And we can feel the fringe of core truths and how our lives are part of them. So, while my sociological practice is usually about understanding the world, it is also about keeping myself in touch with the unknowable essence of human existence that lies beneath.

Practicing sociology is a way to observe the world and to think about and make sense of it. It is also a way to be *in* the world and *of* the world, to play a meaningful role in the life of our species as it shapes and reshapes itself into the mystery of what is going on and what it has to do with us.

Practice What?

Most people probably have some notion of what I mean by 'sociology,' but I doubt that it looks much like sociology as it's practiced. If you've ever looked at a typical introductory sociology text (the only serious glimpse of sociology that most people ever have), you may see sociology as a collection of facts and terms about almost every topic, from the family to economics to politics to crime to religion to the intricacies of conversation. It might remind you of high school social studies, but at a higher level. Looking at all these varied aspects of social life is not by itself sociological, however, because many disciplines examine these same areas. Criminal lawyers, legal scholars, and judges, for example, study crime; economists study economics; political scientists study politics; anthropologists, psychologists, historians, and divorce lawyers study families. But this doesn't mean they are practicing sociology.

This is why vague definitions of sociology as 'about' groups and societies or 'about' social life are not of much use. Since few words are as vague as 'about,' 'sociology' winds up meaning pretty much whatever you want it to mean, which gets close to meaning nothing at all. This makes it easy to think that sociological practice is everywhere, that when the *New York Times* or CNN or PBS or your favorite blog comments on something 'social,' they are practicing sociology. It is also easy to think we can learn as much from surfing the Internet as we can through studying sociology. As a result, many sociologists go out of their way to impress upon people that what they do is more than common sense. They are right, of course; it *is* much more than common sense (now I've said it, too), but having to convince people that it is more than common sense is a situation that sociologists have largely brought on themselves, digging a hole with one hand while trying to fill it in with the other.

You also won't find a clear sense of sociology by looking at scholarly journals. It's not that the authors aren't practicing sociology, but that they're so far removed from caring to explain the *essence* of what they are doing that it gets buried beneath layers of data and theory, implicit rather than out in the open. Since most sociologists write primarily for one another, they seem to assume that the question of what sociology really amounts to isn't worth figuring out, much less articulating so that people outside the field can understand it. You could read several years' worth of journal articles without getting a clue as to what makes them all sociological.

For some sociologists, the lack of a clear sense of sociology's definition is not so much a problem as it is the nature of things. There is no one sociology, they argue, but instead a diversity of sociolo*gies*. It is futile, even presumptuous, to look for a grand narrative that explains everything in one fell swoop. It's old-fashioned, rigid, and overly modernist. Even worse, it won't work.

It is undeniable that sociology encompasses a dazzling collection of ideas and methods and points of interest, and it is undoubtedly true that no theory can explain everything. But if the nature of things is that sociology revolves around many different 'narratives,' *we still have to ask ourselves what it is about these narratives that justifies calling them all sociological.* If we cannot answer that in a reasonably clear and straightforward way, then it's hard to see why anyone would take sociological practice seriously. Without a way to grasp the defining essence of what sociologists do and why they do it, all the research and theory in the world won't amount to much except to sociologists themselves.

That is why I have written this book. The premise for *The Forest and the Trees* is a hypothetical situation I put myself in when I started writing it: if sociology could teach everyone just *one* thing, if it could pass along just *one* central insight, what would that be? Would it be something about the family? About political institutions? About social inequality? About the use of language in social interaction? About conflict theory, exchange theory, functionalism, postmodernism, or any of the other theoretical perspectives sociologists have used over the years? Would it, in short, be some piece of data or a term or a theory from the mountain of data, terms, and theories that fall under the general heading of 'sociology'?

I do not think so, or, at least, I hope not. Far simpler and more powerful is a core idea that serves as a starting point, a gateway opening onto questions that in turn point toward everything else. By itself, such an idea does not explain anything (that wouldn't be the point). Instead, it defines a core view of reality on which sociological practice of all kinds is based, consciously or not, and provides a touchstone for what it means to do it.

When I say that I practice sociology, I refer to that core view, that common ground that joins so many different kinds of work. This book is one practicing sociologist's answer to the hypothetical, the core insight with the greatest potential and promise to transform how we see the world and ourselves in it. This book is about what that core view is and why it matters that we understand it, use it, live it, and pass it on.

1

The Forest, the Trees, and the One Thing

In practicing sociology, I often work in universities, schools, and other organizations with people who are trying to deal with issues of privilege and oppression organized around various differences that occur among human beings, often referred to as 'diversity.' In the simplest sense, diversity is about the variety of people in the world, the varied mix of gender, race, age, social class, disability status, ethnicity, religion, and other social characteristics. In the United States, for example, the population is rapidly changing as a result of immigration from Asia and Latin America.

If the changing mix were all that diversity amounted to, there wouldn't be a problem, since differences make life interesting and enhance creativity. Compared with homogeneous groups, for example, diverse groups are usually better at dealing with problems that require creative solutions. To be sure, diversity brings with it such difficulties as language barriers and different ways of doing things that can confuse or irritate people. But humans are the species with the big brain, the adaptable ones who learn quickly, so learning to get along with different kinds of people should not be a problem that we can't handle. Like travelers in a strange land, we can learn about one another and make room for differences and even figure out how to make good use of them.

As most people know, however, in the world as it is, difference amounts to more than just variety. Difference is also used as a basis for including some and excluding others, for rewarding some more and others less, for treating some with respect and dignity and some as if they were less than fully human or not even there. Difference is used as a basis for privilege, from reserving for some the human dignity that everyone should have to the extreme of deciding who lives and who dies.[1] The resulting patterns of inequality and oppression not only ruin countless people's lives but also create division and resentment fed by injustice and suffering that profoundly affect what happens everywhere from communities, workplaces, and schools to families and the intimacy of marriage.

There are places where the importance of feeling accepted and valued for who you are and what you can do is taken seriously. One way to bring this about is to run programs to help people see the consequences of what is really going on, how those consequences affect people in different ways, and what they can do to create something better. The hardest thing about this work is that people are reluctant to talk about privilege, especially those who belong to privileged groups. When the subject of race and racism comes up, for example, white people often withdraw into silence, as if they are paralyzed by guilt or other feelings they don't dare express. Or they push back, angry and defensive, as if they were being personally attacked and blamed for something they didn't do.

This is what happened in 2005, when the city of New Orleans was devastated by Hurricane Katrina. In the aftermath, thousands of people were left stranded in the city, without adequate water, food, or shelter, and no one who watched the news could fail to notice that those left behind were overwhelmingly people of color. In the weeks that followed, as the slowness of the federal response to the disaster and its victims deepened the level of misery and turned a natural disaster into a national disgrace, some people tried to begin a national dialogue about race and class in the United States. Almost immediately, however, the idea that the unmistakable racial patterns in New Orleans had anything to do with race provoked a storm of denial and even outrage from many in the white population, from President George W. Bush on down, with a large majority reporting the belief that what happened in New Orleans had *nothing* to do with race.[2]

Because members of privileged groups often react negatively to the idea of looking at privilege and oppression, women, black people, Latinos and Latinas, gays, lesbians, people with disabilities, workers, and other subordinate groups may not bring it up. They know how easily privilege can be used to retaliate against them for challenging the status quo and making people feel uncomfortable. So, rather than look at the reality of privilege and oppression, the typical pattern is to choose between two equally futile alternatives: to be stuck in cycles of guilt, blame, and defensiveness or to avoid talking about issues of privilege at all. Either way, the destructive patterns and their consequences continue.

Why does this continue? A major reason is that people tend to think only in terms of individuals, as if a society or a university were nothing more than a collection of people living in a particular time and place. Many writers have pointed out how individualism affects social life by isolating us from one another, promoting divisive competition, and making it harder to sustain a sense of community, that we're all in this together. But individualism does more than affect how we participate in social life. It also affects how we *think* about social life and how we make sense of it.

If we think everything begins and ends with individuals—our personalities, life stories, feelings, and behavior—then it's easy to think that social problems must come down to flaws in individual character. If our society has a drug problem, it must be because individuals just can't or won't say no to drugs. If there is racism, sexism, heterosexism, classism, and other forms of privilege and oppression, it must be due to people who have a personal need to behave in racist, sexist, and other oppressive ways. If there is terrorism in the world, it must be because of certain kinds of people—terrorists—who by their nature feel compelled to engage in terrorist behavior. And if the U.S. Congress can't get anything done, something must be wrong with the senators and representatives. In short, bad things happen because of bad people.

If we think about the world in this way—which is especially common in the United States—then it's not hard to see why members of privileged groups become upset when they are asked to look at the benefits that go along with belonging to that particular group and the price those benefits require other groups to pay. When women, for example, talk about how sexism affects them, individualistic thinking encourages men to hear this as a personal attack: "If women are oppressed, then I must be an evil oppressor who wants to oppress them." Since no man wants to see himself as a bad person, and since most men probably do not consciously intend to act in oppressive ways toward women, men may feel unfairly accused.

In the United States, the idea of individualism goes back to the eighteenth century and, beyond that, to the European Enlightenment and the certainties of modernist thinking. In this period, the rational mind of the individual person was recognized and elevated to a dominant position in the hierarchy of things, separated from and placed above even religion and God. The roots of individualistic thinking in the United States trace in part to the work of William James, who helped pioneer the field of psychology. Later, the importance of individualism was deepened in Europe and the United States by Sigmund Freud's revolutionary insights into the existence of the subconscious and the inner world of individual experience. Over the course of the twentieth century, the life of the individual emerged as a dominant framework for understanding the complexities and mysteries of human existence.

We can see the tendency toward individualism in bookstores and best-seller lists that abound with promises to change the world through self-help and paths to individual growth and transformation. Even on the grand scale of societies—from war and politics to global financial meltdowns—individualism reduces everything to the personalities and behavior of the people we perceive to be in charge. If ordinary people in capitalist societies feel deprived and insecure, then the individualistic answer is that the people who run corporations are greedy or the politicians are corrupt and incompetent. The same perspective argues that poverty exists because of the habits, attitudes, and skills of individual poor people, who are blamed for what they supposedly lack in character and motivation and told to change if they want anything better for themselves.

From an individualistic perspective, the way to make a better world is to put the 'right people' in charge, or to make better people by liberating human consciousness in a New Age, by changing how children are socialized, or by locking up or getting rid of people who will not or cannot be better than they are. Psychotherapy is offered as a model for how to change not only the inner lives of individuals but also the world they live in. If enough people heal themselves through therapy, then the world will 'heal' itself as well.

The solution to collective problems, such as poverty or natural disasters or terrorism, then becomes a matter not of collective solutions but of an accumulation of individual solutions. If we want to have less poverty in the world, the individualistic answer lies in raising people out of poverty or keeping them from becoming poor by changing what sort of people they are, *one person at a time.* Or the way to end mass murders, such as the 2014 killings in Isla Vista, California, is to identify all the individuals who might be inclined to carry out such acts—through mental-health screening, for example—and then somehow stop them before it is too late.

Individualism, then, is a way of thinking that encourages us to explain the world in terms of what goes on inside individuals *and nothing else*. We have been able to think this way through the human ability to be reflexive, which is to say that we have learned to look at ourselves as *selves* with greater awareness and insight than before. We can think about what kind of people we are and how we live in the world, and we can imagine ourselves in new ways. To reimagine ourselves, however, we first have to believe that we exist as distinct individuals apart from the groups, communities, and societies that make up our social environment.

In other words, the *idea* of the individual has to exist for us to think about ourselves as individuals, and the idea of the individual has been around for only a few centuries. Today, we have gone far beyond this by thinking of the social environment itself as just a collection of individuals, of a society as people and of people as society, and of the key to understanding social life as merely understanding what makes the individual tick.

If you grow up and live in a society that is dominated by individualistic thinking, the idea that society is just people seems obvious. The problem with this approach is that it ignores the difference between the individual people who participate in social life and the relationships that connect them to one another and to groups and societies. It is true that you cannot have a social relationship without people to participate and make it happen, but the people and the relationship are not the same thing.

That is why the title of this book plays on the old saying about missing the forest for the trees. In one sense, a forest is simply a collection of individual trees, but it is more than that. It is also a collection of trees that exist in a *particular relation* to one another, and you cannot tell what that relation is by looking at the individual trees. Take a thousand trees and scatter them across the Great Plains of North America, and all you have are a thousand trees. But take those same trees and put them close together, and now you have a forest. The same individual trees in one case constitute a forest and in another are just a lot of trees.

The 'empty space' that separates individual trees from one another is not a characteristic of any one tree or the characteristics of all the individual trees somehow added together. It is something more than that, and it is crucial to understand the *relationships among* trees that make a forest what it is. Paying attention to that 'something more'—whether it is a family or a society or the entire world—and how people are related to it lies at the heart of what it means to practice sociology.

The One Thing

If sociology could teach everyone just one thing with the most profound effect on how we understand social life, it would, I believe, be this: *we are always participating in something larger than ourselves, and if we want to understand social life and what happens to people in it, we have to understand what it is that we are participating in and how we are participating in it.* In other words, the key to understanding social life is neither just the forest nor just the trees but the forest *and* the trees and the consequences that result from their dynamic relationship to each other.

The larger things we participate in are called social systems, which come in all shapes and sizes. In general, the concept of a 'system' refers to any collection of parts or elements that are connected in ways that coalesce into some kind of whole. We can think of the engine in a car as a system, for example, a collection of parts arranged in ways that make the car go. Or we can think of a language as a system, with words and punctuation and rules for how to combine them into sentences that have meaning. We can also think of a family as a system—a collection of elements related to one another in a way that leads us to think of it as a unit. These include such things as the positions of mother, father, wife, husband, spouse, partner, parent, child, daughter, son, sister, and brother. Elements also include shared ideas that tie those positions together to make relationships, such as how 'good mothers' are supposed to act in relation to children or what a family is and what makes family members related to one another as kin. If we combine the positions and ideas and other elements, then we can think of the result as a social system.

In similar ways, we can think of colleges or societies as social systems. They differ from one another—and from families—in the kinds of elements they include and how those are arranged in relation to one another. Colleges and universities have such positions as student, president, and professor, for example, but the position of 'mother' is not part of the academic system. People who work or study in colleges and universities can certainly be mothers, but that is not a position that connects them to those systems.

Such differences are a key to how systems work and produce different kinds of consequences. Corporations are sometimes referred to as families, for example, but if we look at how families and corporations are actually constructed as systems, we can see how unrealistic such notions are. Families usually don't lay off their members when times are tough or when they want to boost the bottom line, and they usually don't divide the food on the dinner table according to who's the strongest and best able to grab the lion's share for themselves.[3] But corporations dispense with workers all the time as a way to raise dividends and the value of stock, and top managers routinely take a huge share of each year's profits even while putting other members of the corporate 'family' out of work.

What social life comes down to, then, is a dynamic relationship between social systems and the people who participate in them. Note that people *participate* in systems without being *parts* of the systems themselves. In this sense, 'father' and 'grandfather' are positions in my family, and I, Allan, am an individual person who actually occupies those positions. It is in this sense that I 'am' a grandfather. This distinction is easy to lose sight of, but it is crucial. It's easy to lose sight of because we are so used to thinking solely in terms of individuals. It is crucial because it means that people are not systems and systems are not people, and if we forget that, we are likely to focus on the wrong thing in trying to solve our problems.

To see the difference between people and systems, imagine that you are in a social situation, such as a church wedding, and someone who has never been in this particular place walks in the door and looks around. Perhaps the visitor is a woman whose car has broken down, and she is looking for a phone so that she can call for help. Most likely, she will know immediately where she is in a social sense and, even more important, will have an accurate idea of what the people in the room expect of her *even though she has no personal knowledge of them whatsoever.* So long as the visitor can accurately identify the social system in which she is participating and her position in it, she will be able to behave appropriately without violating the expectations that go with that situation.

Thinking of systems as just people is why members of privileged groups often take it personally when someone points out that their society is racist or sexist. "The United States is a racist society that privileges whites over people of color," for example, is a statement that describes the United States as a social system. It does *not* thereby describe the individual people who live there, which has more to do with how each of us participates in this society.

As an individual, for example, I cannot avoid participating in this society in one way or another, and I cannot help but be affected and shaped by that. But how all that plays out in practice depends on many things, including the choices I make about *how* to participate. I was born in 1946 and grew up listening to the radio shows of the day, including *Amos 'n' Andy*, which was full of racist stereotypes about black people (the actors were white). Like any other child, I looked to my environment to define what was 'funny.' Since this show was clearly defined as funny from a white perspective in a white-dominated society, and since I was born into a white family, I laughed with everyone else as we drove along listening to the car radio. I even learned to do the voices of 'black' characters and could entertain my family with renditions of classic lines from the show.

Many years later, those racist images are firmly lodged in my memory, because once they get in, there is no getting them out. With the benefit of hindsight, I can see the racism in them and how they are connected to massive injustice and suffering in the society I grew up in and participate in today. As an individual, I cannot undo the past and I cannot undo my childhood. I can, however, choose what to do about race and racism now. I cannot make my society or the place where I live suddenly nonracist, but I can decide how to live as a white person in relation to the privileged position of 'white person' that I occupy. I can decide whether to laugh or object when I hear racist jokes. I can decide how to treat people who are not classified as white. I can decide what to do about the consequences that racism produces, whether to be part of the solution or just part of the problem. I do not feel guilty because my country is racist, because the creation of racism in this country was not my doing. But as a white person who participates in that society, I feel responsible to consider what to do about it. The only way to get past the potential for guilt and see how I can make a difference is to realize that the system is not I, nor am I the system.

Nonetheless, systems and people are closely connected to each other, and seeing how that connection works is a basic part of sociological practice. One way to see this is to compare social systems to a game such as Monopoly, which we can also think of as a social system. The game has positions (players, banker), it has a material reality (the board, the pieces, the dice, play money, property deeds, houses and hotels), and it has ideas that connect those elements in a set of relationships. Specific values define the point of the game—to win—and rules spell out what winning consists of and what's allowed in pursuit of it, including the idea of cheating.

Notice that we can describe the game without saying anything about the personalities, intentions, attitudes, or other characteristics of the people who might play it. The game, in other words, is something that we can describe all by itself, and it exists regardless of whether anyone is playing it at the moment. The same is true of all social systems. We don't have to describe actual senators and representatives, for example, to describe the U.S. Congress as a social system whose characteristics distinguish it from other systems.

I don't play Monopoly anymore, mostly because I don't like the way I behave when I do. When I used to play Monopoly, I would try to win, even against my children, and I couldn't resist feeling good when I did (we're *supposed* to feel good) even if I also felt bad about it. Why did I act and feel this way? It wasn't because I have a greedy, mercenary personality, because I don't behave this way when I'm not playing Monopoly. Clearly I am *capable* of behaving this way as a human being, which is part of the explanation. But the rest of the explanation comes down to the fact that I behave that way because taking all the money and property for yourself is what the game of Monopoly is about.

When I participate in the Monopoly system, greedy behavior is presented to me as a path of least resistance, what I am supposed to do if I want to feel that I belong. And when I play the game, I feel obliged to follow its rules and pursue the values it promotes. I look upon the game as having authority over the people who play it, which becomes apparent when I consider how rare it is for people to suggest changing the rules ("I'm sorry, honey," I say as I take my kid's last dollar, "but that's just the way the game is played"). If *we* were the game, then we would feel free to play by any rules we liked. But we tend not to see games—or systems—in that way. We see them as external to us and therefore not ours to shape in any way we want.

What happens when people participate in a social system depends on two things: the system and how it is organized, and what people actually do as they participate in it from one moment to the next. What people do depends in part on the positions they occupy in relation to other people in the system (in Monopoly, everyone occupies the same position—player—but a classroom includes teachers and students, and a corporation can have hundreds if not thousands of positions). People are what make a system happen. Without their participation, a system exists only as an idea with a physical reality attached. If no one plays Monopoly, it is just a bunch of stuff in a box with rules written inside the cover. And if no one plays Toyota Motor

Company,' it is just a bunch of factories and offices and equipment and rules and accounts written on paper and stored in computers. In a similar sense, a society may be organized in ways that promote racist or sexist outcomes, but for these consequences to happen—or not—someone has to do or not do something in relation to someone else in the context of one social system or another within that society.

For its part, a system affects how we think, feel, and behave as participants. It does this not only through the general process of socialization but also by laying out paths of least resistance in social situations. At any given moment, we could do an almost infinite number of things, but we typically do not realize this and see only a narrow range of possibilities. What the range looks like depends on the system we are in.

While playing Monopoly, for example, I *could* reach over and take money from the bank whenever I want. Or when someone I like lands on a property I own, I *could* say that I'll give them a break and not collect the rent but then happily collect it when someone I don't like lands there. But people would probably object that I wasn't playing 'fair' or by the rules. Since I would rather people not be angry with me or kick me out of the game, it's easier to follow the rules even when I'd rather not. And so I usually do, following the path of least resistance that's presented to people who occupy the same position I occupy in that particular system.

This is why people might laugh at racist or heterosexist jokes even when they make them feel uncomfortable—in that situation, to not laugh and risk being ostracized by everyone may make them feel even *more* uncomfortable. The easiest—although not necessarily easy—choice is to go along. This does not mean we *have to* go along or that we *will*, only that if we do go along, we'll run into less resistance than if we don't.

In other situations, paths of least resistance might look quite different, and giving a friend a break or objecting to racist humor might be seen as just what we're supposed to do. In relation to my children, for example, I'm supposed to do whatever I can to help them—that is the path of least resistance that goes with the relation between parent and child in the family system (except, perhaps, when we're playing Monopoly). However, I'd never want my daughter or son to be a student in one of my classes, because then I'd have to choose between conflicting paths of least resistance associated with two different systems. As a teacher, I'm supposed to treat my students the same, but as a father, I'm supposed to favor my children above other people's children. The path of least resistance in one system is a path of

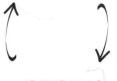

SOCIAL SYSTEMS

We make social
systems happen.

As we participate in
systems, our lives are
shaped by *socialization*
and *paths of least
resistance.*

INDIVIDUALS

Figure 1. Individuals and social systems: A dynamic relationship.

much greater resistance in the other, producing what sociologists call 'role conflict.'[4]

Social systems and people are connected through a dynamic relationship, pictured in Figure 1. People make systems happen—consciously or not—and systems contain paths of least resistance that shape how people participate. Neither people nor systems exist without the other, and yet neither can be reduced *to* the other. The complexity of my life is not some predictable product of the systems I participate in, nor is a social system an accumulation of my own and other people's lives.

What results from all this are patterns of social life and the consequences they produce for people, for systems themselves, and for the world—in short, most of what matters in the human scheme of things and beyond to the Earth and other species affected by how we live. When we can identify how a system is organized, we can see what is likely to result if people follow the paths of least resistance. We know, for example, where the game of Monopoly is going just by reading the rules of the game. We don't have to know anything about the individuals who play it, except the likelihood that most of them will follow the path of least resistance most of the time.

On the surface, the idea that we are always participating in something larger than ourselves may seem fairly simple. But like many ideas that seem simple at first, it can take us to places that transform how we look at the world and ourselves in relation to it.

The Individualistic Model Doesn't Work

Probably the most important basis for sociological practice is that the individualistic perspective that dominates current thinking about social life is wrong. Everything we do or experience happens in relation to a social context of some kind. When a wife and husband argue about who will clean the bathroom, for example, or who will take care of a sick child when they both work outside the home, the issue is never simply about the two of them, although it may seem so at the time. We have to ask about the larger context in which something occurs.

We might ask, for example, how this instance is related to living in a society organized in ways that privilege men over women, in part by not making men feel obliged to share equally in domestic work except when they choose to 'help out.' On an individual level, he may think she's being a nag, while she may think he's being a selfish jerk. But the issue is never as simple as that, because what both may miss is that in a different kind of society, they might not be having this argument in the first place, because both might feel obliged to take care of home and children.

In similar ways, when we see ourselves as a unique result of the family we came from, we overlook how each family is connected to larger patterns. The emotional problems we struggle with as individuals, for example, are not due simply to what kind of parents we had, for their participation in social systems—at work, in the community, in religion, in society as a whole—shaped them as people, including their roles as mothers and fathers. An individualistic model is misleading, because it encourages us to explain human behavior and experience from a perspective so narrow that it misses most of what is happening.

A related problem is that we cannot understand what goes on in social systems simply by looking at individuals. In one sense, for example, suicide is a solitary act done by an individual, typically while alone.[5] If we ask why people kill themselves, we are likely to think first of how people are feeling when they do it—hopeless, depressed, guilty, lonely, or, in the case of soldiers and suicide bombers, obligated by honor, duty, loyalty, or religious belief to sacrifice themselves for someone else or what they identify as a greater good. That might explain suicides taken one at a time, but what do we have when we add up all the suicides that occur in a society for a given year? What does that number tell us, and, more importantly, about what? This was the question posed by the great French sociologist Émile Durkheim, one of the founders of sociology, in his classic work *Suicide*.

The suicide rate for the entire U.S. population in 2010, for example, was 12 suicides per 100,000 people. If we look inside that number, we find that the rate for males was 20 per 100,000, but the rate for females was only 5 per 100,000. The rate also differs dramatically by race and country and varies over time. The suicide rate for white people in the United States, for example, was higher than that for any other racial group, more than double the rate for black and Latino people and 30 percent higher than the rate for Native Americans. The highest rate for any major demographic group is found among white males.

There are also variations among countries. While the rate in the United States was 12 per 100,000, for example, it was 22 per 100,000 in Hungary but only 6 per 100,000 in Italy. So, in the United States, males and white people are far more likely than females and black people to kill themselves, and people in the United States are twice as likely as Italians to commit suicide but only one-half as likely as Hungarians.[6]

If we use an individualistic model to explain such differences, we tend to see them as nothing more than a sum of individual suicides. If males are more likely to kill themselves, then it must be because males are more likely to feel the emotional states associated with suicidal behavior. In other words, the psychological factors that cause individuals to kill themselves must be more common among males than they are among females or more common among people in the United States than among Italians. There is nothing wrong with such reasoning. It may be exactly right as far as it goes, but that is just the problem—it does not go far enough. It does not answer the question of *why* these differences exist in the first place.

Why, for example, would males be more likely to feel suicidally hopeless and depressed than females, or Hungarians more likely than Italians? Or why would Hungarians who feel suicidally depressed be more likely to go ahead and kill themselves than Italians who feel the same way? To answer such questions, we need more than an understanding of individual psychology. Among other things, we need to pay attention to the fact that such words as 'female,' 'white,' and 'Italian' name positions that people occupy in social systems. Acknowledging this fact draws attention to how those systems work and what it means to occupy those positions in them in relation to paths of least resistance.

Sociologically, a suicide rate is a number that describes something about a group or a society, not the individuals who belong to it. A suicide rate of 12 per 100,000 tells us nothing about you, me, or anyone else. Each of us either commits suicide during a given year or we do not, and the rate cannot tell us who does what. In the same way, how individuals feel before they kill themselves is not by itself enough to explain why some groups or societies have higher suicide rates than others. Individuals can feel depressed or lonely, but groups and societies cannot feel a thing. We could consider that Italians might tend to be less depressed than people in the United States, for example, or that in the United States, people might tend to deal with feelings of depression more effectively than in Hungary. It makes no sense at all, however, to say that the United States is more depressed or lonely than Italy.

While looking at the psychological process in individuals might explain why one person commits suicide, doing so cannot explain *patterns* of suicide found in social systems. To explain systemic patterns, we have to look at how people feel and behave *in relation to* systems and how those systems work. We need to ask, for example, how societies are organized in ways that encourage people who participate in them to experience various psychological conditions or to respond to them in suicidal or nonsuicidal ways. We need to see how belonging to particular social categories shapes people's experience as they participate in social life and how their participation limits the alternatives they think they can choose from. What is it about being male or being white that can make suicide a path of least resistance?

How, in other words, can we go to the heart of sociological practice to ask how people participate in something larger than themselves and see how this affects what they do? How can we see the relationship between people and systems that produces variations in suicide rates or, for that matter, everything else that we do and experience, from having sex to going to work to dying?

Just as we cannot tell what is going on in a system only by looking at individuals, we also cannot tell what is going on in individuals just by looking at systems. Something may look like one thing in the system as a whole but like something else entirely when we look at the people who participate in that system. If we look at the kind of mass destruction and suffering that war and terrorism typically cause, for example, an individualistic model suggests a direct link with the kinds of people who participate in it. If war and terrorism produce cruelty, bloodshed, aggression, and conquest, then the people who participate in such activities must be cruel, bloodthirsty, aggressive people who want to conquer and dominate others. When viewing the carnage and destruction that war and terrorism typically leave in their wake, we are likely to ask, "What kind of people would do such a thing?"

Sociologically, however, the question is misleading, because it reduces a social phenomenon to a simple matter of 'kinds of people' without looking at the systems those people participate in. Since we are always participating in one system or another, when someone crashes an airplane into a building or drops a bomb that incinerates thousands of people, we cannot explain that action simply by figuring out 'what kind of person would do such a thing.'

In fact, if we look at what is known about people who fight in wars, they appear fairly normal by most standards and anything but bloodthirsty and cruel.[7] Most accounts portray the experience of being in combat as alternating between extreme boredom and extreme fright. Soldiers worry much less about glory than they do about not being hurt or killed and getting themselves and their friends home in one piece. For most soldiers, killing and the almost constant danger of being killed are traumatic experiences that leave them forever changed as people. They go to war not in response to some inner need to be aggressive and kill but because they think it is their duty to go, or they see enlisting as a way to be of service to their country, or they have seen war portrayed in books and movies as an adventurous way to prove their manhood (a standard that applies to both men and women in combat), or they do not want to risk family and friends rejecting them for not measuring up as true patriots, or they are afraid of being sent to prison if they refuse to be drafted.

People are not systems and systems are not people, which means that social life can produce horrible or wonderful consequences without necessarily meaning that the people who participate are horrible or wonderful themselves. Good people participate in systems that produce bad consequences all the time. I am often aware of this in the simplest situations, such as when I go to buy clothes, food, or electronics. Many of the clothes sold in the United States, for example, are made in sweatshops, some in the United States, but most in nonindustrial countries, such as Indonesia and Thailand, where people often work under conditions that resemble slavery in many respects or for wages that are so low they can barely live on them. Similarly, many of the fruits and vegetables sold in grocery stores are harvested by migrant farm workers who work under conditions that are not much better. And in 2012, shocking revelations emerged about the treatment of workers in Chinese factories where Apple iPads and iPhones are manufactured. If these workers were provided with decent employment conditions and paid a living wage, the price of clothing, food, and electronics would be significantly higher, which means that I benefit from the daily mistreatment and exploitation of thousands if not millions of people. The fact that I benefit does not make me a bad person, but my participation in that system does involve me in what happens as a result.

It's About Us and It's Not

If we start from the idea that we are always participating in something larger than ourselves and that social life flows from this relationship, then we have to consider that we are all involved—even if indirectly- in the social consequences that result, both the good and the bad. By definition, if I participate in a racist society—no matter what my race—then I am involved in white privilege and the oppression of people of color.

As an individual, I may not feel or act in racist ways, and in my heart I may even hate racism, but that is beside the core sociological point that I am *involved* in one way or another by virtue of my participation in society itself.[8] If the path of least resistance is for people to take what I say or write more seriously because they perceive me as being white, for example, then I am likely to receive a benefit of racism, regardless of whether I'm aware of it. In doing so, I have unwittingly participated in racism. This raises the question of how society works *and* how I participate in it—whether I actively defend white privilege, let people know that I am against racism, or just go about my business and pretend there is no problem to begin with.

From this perspective, it doesn't make sense to use the words 'racist' and 'racism' as nothing more than ways to describe the character of individual people, because the most important factor in perpetuating privilege and oppression is how social systems are organized, including the paths of least resistance they lay down for participants to follow regardless of what kind of people they are.

In his book *Portraits of White Racism*, sociologist David Wellman argues that 'racist' and 'racism' should refer to anything that has the *consequence* of perpetuating white privilege, regardless of the intentions or character of the people whose behavior brings about that result. Most people believe, for example, that it's good for children to go to school in their own neighborhoods. Since racial segregation in housing is still pervasive, however, such a policy also has the consequence of perpetuating racial segregation in schools, which a considerable body of evidence shows is not good for students of any race, but especially for children of color. Those who advocate for neighborhood schools often protest that their position has nothing to do with race, which may be true of their intentions as individuals. But the *consequence* of such a policy has a great deal to do with race and the perpetuation of white privilege and the oppression of people of color that results from that privilege.

Getting clear about the relationship between individuals and social systems can dramatically alter how we see potentially painful issues and ourselves in relation to them. This is especially true for people in privileged groups who otherwise resist looking at the nature and consequences of privilege. Their defensive resistance is probably the biggest single barrier to ending privilege and oppression. Most of the time resistance happens because, like everyone else, people in privileged groups are stuck in an individualistic model of the world and cannot see how to acknowledge white privilege as a fact of social life without also feeling personally to blame for it. And the people who are most likely to feel this way are often the ones who are otherwise most open to doing something to make things better.

When we look at a problem such as racism sociologically, however, we can see how it is both about us and not about us. It is not about us in the sense that we did not create the racist society we all live in. As I was growing up white, for example, no one asked me whether it was okay for white people to use *Amos 'n' Andy* to make fun of black people and keep them in their place beneath white privilege. And if they *had* asked me, I doubt that as a small child I would have known enough to object. In this sense, white people who have grown up in a racist environment have no reason to feel guilty when they hear people express anger about the existence of white racism and the harm and suffering that it causes.

Racism is also about me personally, however, because regardless of whether I am aware of it, I am always making choices about how to participate in a society that is organized in racist ways and that makes behavior that perpetuates white privilege a path of least resistance. Regardless of how I behave, as a white person I am eligible for privilege that comes at the expense of people of other races. As Harry Brod argues:

> We need to be clear that there is no such thing as giving up one's privilege to be "outside" the system. One is always *in* the system. The only question is whether one is part of the system in a way which challenges or strengthens the status quo. Privilege is not something I *take* and which I therefore have the option of *not* taking. It is something that society *gives* me, and unless I change the institutions which give it to me, they will continue to give it, and I will continue to *have* it, however noble and egalitarian my intentions.[9]

Because white privilege is built into the system itself, I don't have to like it or believe in it or even do anything to receive it. When I go shopping at the mall, salespeople and store detectives don't follow me around as if I were going to steal something. They don't swoop down on me and pointedly ask, "Can I help you?" as if I were a suspicious character or something other than a serious customer. But for people of color, such treatment is a common occurrence, and it usually doesn't matter how well they dress or how much money they have to spend.[10]

Most people would agree that everyone should be treated with dignity and respect, but when some are and some are not simply because of which social category they belong to, then an oppressive system of privilege is at work. And whether I like it or not, as a white person I benefit from that by getting something of value that is denied to others. Once I see this, it is hard to avoid asking how I participate in the system that produces such consequences. What are my responsibilities? What could I do differently that would contribute to different outcomes? How can I be part of the solution to racism rather than just part of the problem?

In other words, by making me aware that I am involved in something larger than myself, sociological practice gets me off the hook of personal guilt and blame for a world that I did not create and that is not my fault. At the same time, however, it makes me aware of how I choose to participate in that world and how and why those choices matter. I have no reason to feel guilty simply because I am white, but I also do not have the luxury of thinking that racism and white privilege have nothing to do with me.[11]

Personal Solutions Cannot Solve Social Problems

If the shape of social life is rooted in relationships between people and the systems they participate in, then those relationships are also where social problems will or will not be solved. Personal solutions are just that—personal and individual—and they cannot solve social problems unless they include changes in how people outwardly participate in social systems. An individualistic model encourages us to think that if enough individuals change, then systems will change as well, but a sociological perspective shows why change is not this simple. The problem is that social life is not just a product of people's personal characteristics and behavior, for these arise out of their participation in social systems. In that sense, social life depends on how people are connected to one another through the structures of social relationships, and systems do not change unless relationships change.

An individualistic model also doesn't work in practice, because personal solutions arise primarily from a sense of our own personal needs, and focusing our attention on personal needs is a path of least resistance. Once we find a solution to the problem that works for us personally, we've accomplished our goal and are likely to leave the larger problem behind rather than continue to work on it to help make things better for others.

In the United States, for example, personal solutions are the typical response to the problem of economic insecurity, which seems to be a way of life for the vast majority of people in many capitalist societies, as we saw all too clearly after the financial crisis of 2008. Rather than stop and ask how the economic system itself sets us up to feel insecure, the path of least resistance is to work hard to establish our own private zones of safety within an insecure system, hanging on to what we have while leaving everyone else to fend for themselves.

Not surprisingly, this strategy does not lower the overall level of insecurity and poverty in society as a whole—it does not, in other words, solve these *social* problems. Instead, it shuffles people in and out of various levels of well-being and security, like a game of musical chairs. As long as I have a chair for myself, why raise questions about the fact that there aren't enough chairs to go around?

Sociological practice uses more complex models of change that focus on several different levels of social life at once. Consider, for example, the problem of pollution, which a growing number of communities around the world have to deal with. Suppose that people in your town start getting sick. Large numbers of children don't show up for school, and local clinics and hospital emergency rooms are jammed with patients who turn out to be suffering from chemical toxins.

On a purely individual level, we could say that we have figured out why people are getting sick. And to solve the problem in terms of individuals, we could just treat each sick person until they get well and change people's behavior so that they don't get sick again. If the toxic chemicals are in the water supply, then don't drink the water. Buy bottled water instead. Each person now has a solution to the problem, assuming, of course, they can afford to drink bottled water or install expensive filtration systems in the home. It would probably turn out that, as in most communities, some people would be able to afford the individualist solution and some would not, which means that some people would still get sick. Of course, we might enact some kind of collective response to this inequality by providing subsidies for poor people to buy bottled water, but notice that we still would not have done anything about the underlying problem of polluted water. We would simply have found a way for individual people to avoid the effects of drinking it.

To take the problem to a sociological level, we have to ask about social systems and how people participate in them, and so far we have not said anything about people getting sick as a systemic problem. People are told to change their personal behavior by not drinking water out of the tap. But nothing's been said about the possibility of something larger going on that might require changing the system they are participating in.

Suppose we trace the toxin backward from each faucet and wind up at the local reservoir. From there, we trace it to the surrounding soil and a stream, and from there to a local chemical plant that employs a large number of people in the town. Now we have a different explanation of why people are getting sick and a different solution: get the plant to stop dumping chemical waste in ways that wind up in the town's water supply.

Suppose, however, that the people who run the company say they cannot do that because it would cost too much, and the business they are in is so competitive that they would have to close down the plant and move to where people care more about their jobs than they do about polluted water. And if the owners close down the plant, many local people will lose their jobs, the effects of which will ripple throughout the town as fewer people have money to spend in local businesses or pay in taxes to support schools and other services.

Now the problem of what is making people sick is more than a simple matter of how the plant is run. The problem is also related to larger systems that the plant as a whole participates in and to the company's powerful position in relation to the community that depends on it for jobs. The nature of the economic system—competitive global capitalism—shapes the choices that plant owners make in ways that affect the quality of water that people have to drink. That economic system is tied to unequal distributions of power and wealth and to cultural values about the desirability of making a profit and the right of people to do what they want with private property, perhaps even dumping toxic waste on land they own or in streams that run across their property. Ultimately, the town may have to confront the company's power over the lives of residents and choose between powerful competing values about how communities and societies should work.

Taking the problem to the level of systems does not mean we ignore individuals. It is not a matter of one or the other, because sociological practice looks at social life in relation to systems *and* how people participate in them. People often box themselves into a false choice between attributing a problem to society and blaming it on individuals. But social life doesn't work that way. The choice is hardly ever as simple as one or the other, of society *or* individuals, because societies and individuals exist only in relation to each other. The challenge of sociological practice is to see how this relationship works. If we don't, we go back and forth between acting as if individuals play no part in creating social problems and acting as if people behave in a social vacuum without being affected by the kind of society they live in.

There is a third alternative, which is both/and instead of either/or. Systems do not change without people changing at one point or another, and no system can change through individual change alone.

It's Even Messier and More Interesting

The language of 'systems' and 'individuals' can make things seem a lot simpler and more clear-cut than they really are. It encourages us to think of systems as things, as rigid molds that people must fit into. In some ways, a social system is thinglike in that we can identify characteristics, such as the distribution of power or rules or a physical setting or positions that people occupy as participants. 'School,' for example, conjures up some predictable images—rooms with chairs in rows, cafeterias, gymnasiums, libraries, computer labs, students, teachers, locker-lined hallways, bells ringing at regular intervals, rules, grades, teachers having power over students, administrators having power over teachers, semesters, vacations, teaching, learning, graduation. Because such images of this thing we call 'school' are relatively fixed in our minds, we can experience it as being thinglike.

In other words, we can think of school as something outside of us, as an 'it' rather than a 'me' or an 'us.' People attend or work in 'it,' but the people are not it, and it is not the people. In that way, school is like the game of Monopoly in a box. People take it out (go to school), play it for a while (teach, study, administer), and then put it away (go home). And that is pretty much what it is, or so we might think.

But social life is messier and more interesting than that, because in many ways social systems are not some*thing*. Each is an ongoing process. Social systems are continually being created and re-created as people *do* things to make them *happen*. The associations we have with 'school' are just words on a page, images in our minds, until people actually participate in the process of school as a system. When they do, some familiar patterns shape what goes on, but there is also an enormous amount of variation around those patterns as people put their own spin on how they are going to participate. 'It' never happens in exactly the same way twice, because what we call 'school' is as much about what people do as it is about all the associations we have with the idea of school as a kind of social system.

While we may not be aware of it at the time, at any given moment, any of the people in a school could do something unexpected that would shape how school happens in that time and place. We may have a general understanding of what school is in the same way that we understand what Monopoly is. And we can use such knowledge to predict with some accuracy what the general patterns will look like in a given school on a given day. But there is a great deal that we cannot predict, because in an important sense, 'school' happens only *as* it happens. In this sense, school literally *is* what people do when they identify themselves as 'in school.'

What makes social life and sociological practice messy and interesting is that both ways of looking at things are true. When I visit a college classroom and sit down with students, for example, I can feel how the situation of school limits what I see as my options. I know in general what I'm expected to do and what, therefore, would be considered inappropriate for that situation. But as I sit there looking at the students, there is also a sense in the air of 'So, what are we going to do?' Although we all know that we're in school and that this means many things are very unlikely to happen, we also don't really know what *is* going to happen, because it hasn't happened yet. So, I say something to start things off, or a student asks a question or makes a comment on something they have read, or something else altogether happens. And so it goes from there, as 'school' unfolds, emerging from how *these* people choose from moment to moment what they are going to *make* of their participation in this system.

If we want to explain what happens during that time, it is not enough to understand what school is about as a social system, and it's not enough to understand who the people in the room are as individuals. What happens depends on *both/and*—it depends on *both* the system these people are in *and* how they choose to participate in it.

What makes things still messier and still more interesting is that in important ways, we are not all in the same situation. Because we occupy a variety of social positions within each system, we tend to experience each situation differently. We are shaped differently by it, limited by it in different ways, and therefore tend to participate differently. What school is about, then, varies depending on whether you're a student or a teacher, female or male, Asian American, Native American, white, Chicana, African American, older, younger, working class, lower class, middle class, upper class, immigrant, native-born, heterosexual, bisexual, lesbian, gay, transgender, with or without a disability, employed, unemployed, married, single, with or without children. Such characteristics locate us in different ways in relation to other people and to social systems. They affect how we see ourselves and others, how they see us, and how we treat one another as we participate in making a system happen. When we say that we are always participating in something larger than ourselves, it is important to remember that 'we' is not a homogeneous term. There are multiple we's in social life, and an important part of sociological practice is to see how this affects what happens.

Into the Practice

All forms of sociological practice are 'sociological' because they flow from the same basic questions: what are people participating in and how are they participating in it? The work can vary in the balance it strikes between the two questions, with some work leaning more toward one or the other. A study of how people use language to affect how other people see them, for example, might pay little attention to the social systems where such behavior takes place. Or a study of the world economy might never look at the fine details of how people interact as they participate. But the connections between systems and people are always there for us to follow toward a deeper grasp of the complex web that makes up social life and our experience of it and ourselves. Although the main focus in the rest of this book is on systems, questions about how we figure in social life are never far off, for without people to make systems happen from one moment to the next, there would be no social life to understand or anyone to care one way or another.

The next three chapters lay out a systematic way to think about what makes one system different from another in terms of its cultural, structural, and population/ecological characteristics. Keep a couple of things in mind as you read these chapters. The first is that I've never found a clear, coherent way to describe this approach all at once. I find it easier on the mind to break it into pieces taken one at a time—hence separate chapters on culture, structure, and population/ecology.

The problem with doing it this way is that in reality, the pieces do not occur separately, but only in relation to one another. It is similar to studying human anatomy. There is no nervous system, for example, without a circulatory system, and yet anatomy textbooks devote separate chapters to each system, as If each were a distinct entity existing on its own. To the extent that each system is distinct and separate, it is only so in our minds, since nerves, vessels, and the body are completely bound with one another. We can invent ways of thinking that allow us to *imagine* a circulatory or nervous system as something apart from everything else, but this is only a device, a learning tool that makes things easier to comprehend. As a device, explaining things in this way also raises a challenge by distorting the nature of reality, which I try to put back together later in the book.

The other problem with carving things up is that something has to come first, and it can be tempting to infer a rank of importance from the order in which topics appear, as in 'Culture must be the most important because it comes first.' Thinking that would be a mistake. I begin with culture because as a writer and a thinker, I am drawn to words and symbols and how humans construct reality in their minds. I have a special affinity for culture, so that is where I begin, knowing all the while that everything is connected to everything else in complex ways that require us to grasp not only the parts but also the whole, to which we turn in Chapter 7.

2

Culture

Symbols, Ideas, and the Stuff of Life

As I sit in my office—which happens to be in the house where I live—and type these words, I hear a loud rumbling sound from beyond the window. I stop and look out to see a darkening western sky. In the narrowest sense, when I say, "I hear," all that means is that whatever makes the 'sound' does so by making the air move. The moving air hits my eardrums and makes them vibrate, and a complex mechanism in the ear turns the vibration into an electrical impulse. The impulse goes to my brain, which then has the experience of 'hearing' a sound. And when I 'see' a darkening sky, all that happens is that light enters my eye, where it is converted to electrical impulses that go to my brain, which turns them into something I experience as a visual image. Of course, the process doesn't stop there, because almost immediately a string of words flashes across my consciousness: "Uh-oh, thunder." Then more words: "It's gonna rain in the upstairs windows." I go upstairs and close the windows. More words: "I'd better turn off my computer so it doesn't get zapped by lightning." I turn it off, unplug it, and go watch out the window. But no lightning flashes, and no rain falls. The western sky gradually clears. "False alarm," I say to myself, and I go back to writing.

What just happened illustrates a basic aspect of social life that makes it possible. My body had a series of experiences—vibrations hitting my ears, light entering my eyes, electrical impulses going to my brain. But I did not leave it at that, as I used words to make sense of the vibrations and the light.

I named the rumble 'thunder' and the dark sky 'rain clouds,' and together they became in my mind a thunder and lightning storm on its way. By themselves, the sensations did not make me do anything. I *responded* to the words and what they meant to me.

When I used words to make what I heard and saw mean something, I constructed a reality on top of the physical sensations. I started thinking about what *might* happen even though it wasn't actually happening at the time. 'The storm' existed only in my imagination and in the words I used to think about it and the damage it might cause. My behavior was based entirely on what I thought. I know this because if I had thought different words—such as, 'The gods are angry and it's me they're angry at'—I would have acted quite differently.

We tend to think that we live in the world as it 'really' is. When I hear a rumble and think 'thunder,' it doesn't occur to me in that moment that I'm involved in a creative process. I don't realize that I am *choosing* a word and using it to attach a particular meaning to the sound. Instead, I act as though the word and the sound are one and the same thing—that is, the sound *is* 'thunder.'

In other words, the reality that really matters to me is not the sound itself—the moving air that hits my eardrum—but the words and ideas I use to describe that reality and make it mean something. And that reality is something I carry inside my head. If I used different words to describe the sound—say, 'suicide bomber'—I would create a different reality. I don't mean that I create the sound itself when I name it. It is whatever it is. What I do construct is what I think the sound *means* and therefore what it *is* to me, and I use words to do so.

Where do I get the words and the ideas that go along with them that prompt me to do one thing rather than another? The answer is that I participate in a society that has a *culture*, and that culture contains words and ideas that people use to name and interpret what they experience. If I lived in a different society with a different culture, then I might have associated that sound with ideas about supernatural beings rather than simply 'weather.' But I don't, and so I didn't.

One of the most remarkable things about human beings is our ability to use culture to create the world we actually live in, to make up our world from scratch. Most of what we take for reality consists not of things as they 'really' are but of ideas people have developed *about* things as they *think* they are. Culture is where all those ideas wind up, and culture is what we look to for the tools we need to make sense of things, including ourselves.

Constructing Reality

Every social system has a culture. A college class has one. So does the Internet, and so does Canada. Culture consists primarily of symbols—especially the words contained in language—and various kinds of ideas that shape how we think about everything from relationships with other people to the meaning of life. It also includes such practices as music, art, dance, and religious rituals. It includes how we shape the physical world around us, from using sand to make silicon that goes into computer chips to building cities to arranging flowers and plants in that familiar form known as a garden. Culture is both material (the physical 'stuff' of social life) and nonmaterial (the symbols and ideas we use to think and give meaning to just about everything).

Symbols make culture possible, because they are what we use to give something meaning beyond what it otherwise 'is.' Symbols are building blocks that we use to make sentences, and sentences are what make such ideas as 'Thunder means a storm is coming' or 'Capitalism is the best economic system in the world.' In the simplest sense, when we give something a name—such as 'thunder'—we create a relationship with it by making it have something to do with us. If we do not have a name for it, we tend not to notice it and not live in relation to it. It doesn't 'matter.' When we call a dot of light in the sky a 'star,' for example, we make it part of a cultural reality. In that sense, we make it real to us in ways that it otherwise wouldn't be, even though that dot of light would still exist up there in the sky.

As a species, we miss most of what is around us because there is so much of it and it's impossible to pay attention to more than a tiny portion of it. We use symbols to name things as a way to focus our attention and build a reality to live in. As philosopher Susanne Langer puts it, using symbols to construct reality lies at the heart of what makes us human:

Only a small part of reality, for a human being, is what is actually going on; the greater part is what he imagines in connection with the sights and sounds of the moment. . . . It means that his world is bigger than the stimuli which surround him, and the measure of it is the reach of his coherent and steady imagination. An animal's environment consists of the things that act on his senses. . . . He does not live in a world of unbroken space and time, filled with events even when he is not present or when he is not interested; his "world" has a fragmentary, intermittent existence, arising and collapsing with his activities. A human being's world hangs together, its events fit into each other; no matter how devious their connections, there always are connections, in one big framework of time and space. . . . *The world* is something human.[1]

Before going any further, notice the words Langer uses in this passage to refer to people. Every time she uses a pronoun to refer to human beings, it is a masculine 'he,' 'him,' or 'his.' She never uses feminine pronouns or gender-neutral pronouns, such as 'they' or 'them.' Imagine that she had written the passage in this way:

Only a small part of reality, for human beings, is what is actually going on; the greater part is what they imagine in connection with the sights and sounds of the moment. . . . It means that their world is bigger than the stimuli which surround them, and the measure of it is the reach of their coherent and steady imagination. An animal's environment consists of the things that act on the senses. . . . Animals do not live in a world of unbroken space and time, filled with events even when they are not present or when they are not interested; their "world" has a fragmentary, intermittent existence, arising and collapsing with their activities. A human being's world hangs together, its events fit into each other; no matter how devious their connections, there always are connections, in one big framework of time and space. . . . *The world* is something human.

In the first version, men are explicitly included by equating 'human' with 'male,' while women are not. Since words are what we use to construct reality, what is the reality these words help construct? They construct a world in which men and their actions are at the center of attention (male-centered) and in which men are used as the standard against which 'human' is measured and judged (male-identified). They also help construct a world in which women are relatively invisible and thereby devalued and subordinate (male-dominated). It is easy for me as a man to see myself in the first version, but for a woman to see herself, she has to make a mental leap between what are clearly masculine pronouns to a thought like, "Well, it really means people in general, which includes me, since I'm a person." As a man, I don't have to go through those mental gymnastics to locate myself in what we call 'humanity,' and that simplicity is part of male privilege in a patriarchal world.

Rather than rush to fault Langer for her use of language, it is important to note that she is writing this passage in 1962, in a society whose culture offered little that would make her aware of what she was doing. She is using language as most people around her used it and creates a reality in her prose that fits comfortably with the reality of the society she lived and wrote in, a society in which male privilege and the oppression of women played a prominent role in everyday life. Male privilege, of course, is still alive and well, but since Langer's writing of these words, various women's movements have managed to shift the political landscape and distribution of power enough to create a greater awareness of the dynamics of gender. As a result, what Langer 'sees' when she is writing in 1962 is different from what I 'see' when I read her words now, which is precisely her point and mine.

We can use language to construct all kinds of reality, including what we cannot experience through our senses. We cannot hear or smell or touch what we call love, for example, like we can a banana. We can see how people treat us, and we might interpret that behavior to mean they love us, but the behavior itself is not love. The behavior is what we take to *mean* that the person loves us. What we call love is something we think exists beneath what we can see and hear. Love is about how people see us and think and feel about us, none of which we can actually observe directly. Someone can say, "I love you" or "I feel deeply for you," but the words are not the love or the feeling. They are *about* the love and the feeling.

We use words to construct something we take to be real—the person loves us—and, most importantly, we act as though what we have created is as real as a chair or a piano. And although—or perhaps because—we cannot see or hear what the words represent, we may organize our lives around getting someone to say them to us and prove they really mean what they seem.

Unlike love, an atom is something scientists may be able to see someday, but even if they do, for most people it won't exist except as an idea about what the word 'atom' supposedly represents. Before the word was coined, what we now think of as the atom simply did not exist for anyone. Now, however, an atom is real for anyone who has ever taken a high school science class, even though we have never actually seen one. All we've seen are words written by people who claim that atoms exist, and the words are enough to construct what we then take to be reality. There is this object that I cannot see and never will, but a word that names it somehow connects me to it. I can think of my hand, for example, or my dog as something composed of atoms. It is this way with all the words that we use, like slender threads connecting us to whatever they point to and name. The words weave a reality and then connect us to it.

In this sense, the power of symbols goes far beyond labeling things—this is a sugar maple tree, this is love, this is Einstein's theory of relativity. Symbols are also what we use to feel connected to a reality outside ourselves. Without symbols, a great deal of what we 'know' and experience would not exist for us. There would be no memory of what we call the past, except in the form of sensations, such as visual imagery or smells. There would be no thinking in the present and no wondering about what we call the future.

Not only would we lose most of our connection to our own past experience, but we would also have no way to share in the experience of others. This is essentially what storytelling traditions are about in many societies and what history is about in others. Back in the 1970s, for example, in my introductory sociology class, I described the 1968 Democratic Presidential Convention in Chicago to illustrate how people can perceive the same event in different ways, depending on the position they occupy in the social system. Massive antiwar demonstrations took place in Chicago, and the confrontations between demonstrators and police resulted in mayhem and violence. As I watched the events unfold on live television, it seemed to me that the police were rioting and out of control as they attacked nonviolent demonstrators. But when I picked up the next day's edition of a Chicago newspaper, the headlines announced a riot by antiwar demonstrators that was put down by courageous police officers doing their duty.[2]

In my early years of teaching, I needed to only mention the 1968 Democratic Convention for my students to know what I was talking about. But as time passed, there came a day when my new class just sat there without a flicker of recognition. They had no idea what I was talking about, and so I had to tell them a story, string out a river of words to connect them to something that happened beyond their own experience. I had to construct something that they could then look upon as a chunk of reality, knowing, of course, that a Chicago police officer might have told them a very different story. Later, if someone mentioned the 1968 Democratic Convention, my students could say, "I know about that," even though they were not there or even alive when it happened. That event became real to them, where before it did not even exist. And mere words made it so.

Beliefs: "I'll See It When I Believe It"

The first purpose of every culture is to provide a way to know what to consider true and what to consider false, and this is what beliefs are about. Notice the difference between 'what to *consider* true' and 'what *is* true,' since what is treated as truth in one culture or historical period may be dismissed as myth, fantasy, or propaganda in another. In Christianity and Judaism, for example, the idea that God exists is obviously true, but for Zen Buddhists, Confucians, and animists, the idea of God is not part of religious life or anything else.

In a sense, symbols are the simplest kind of belief statement, for every dictionary definition declares that something or other is real and exists. If there is a word for something, we are much more likely to see and treat it as real. As recently as a century ago, for example, the word 'homosexual' was never used to describe a kind of person, as in 'He's a homosexual.' It was used instead to describe a kind of sexual behavior without indicating something about a person's social identity. In that sense, homosexuals did not exist, although many people engaged in homosexual behavior of one kind or another. Where before people saw only sexual behavior, now people are more likely to see 'gays,' 'lesbians,' 'bisexuals,' and 'straights' as distinct types of people.

Such changes don't just come out of the blue but accompany a shift in social relationships, in this case serving as a basis for privileging heterosexuals above everyone else—an arrangement that is closely related to male privilege. As a result, what people see now differs from what people saw then, because the cultural truth of sexual orientation today looks quite different from the truth of sexual orientation then.

Our dependence on beliefs to determine what is real turns on its head the old expression 'I'll believe it when I see it' or its equivalent, 'Seeing is believing.' 'I'll see it when I believe it' may be closer to the way things really are.

When we string words together to make more complex beliefs, we fashion the world and our place in it. Unlike many Native American cultures, for example, typical European-based cultures see humans and animals as altogether different. The 'natural world' and what goes on in it do not include humans. Birds building nests are doing something 'natural,' but people building houses are not. The distinction is completely arbitrary, since in each case a species is using its natural abilities to make something that suits it. The fact that we can use our opposable thumbs to manipulate such objects as hammers and nails or our brains to invent physics and engineering is no less natural than a beaver's ability to chew tree trunks clean through or design a lodge that can withstand a flood.

In Western cultures, however, there is nature on the one hand and humanity on the other, a kind of denial that sets us up to see ourselves as separate from other living things. Such denial justifies a controlling and exploitative relationship between humans and the rest of the natural world and gets us into a lot of trouble by encouraging us to live as though we have no deep roots in our environment, the Earth, and the cycles of nature. It encourages us to think of ourselves as above the 'laws of nature' (since we are not part of nature) and to suppose that we can get away with things that other species cannot. We act as though we can pollute the environment with chemicals and waste, destroy the ozone layer in the atmosphere and fill it with greenhouse gases that raise global temperatures, exhaust the soil, and cut down the forests and still survive and even prosper as other species go extinct all around us. Such arrogance makes us dangerous not only to other species but also to ourselves. We may not *believe* we are animals that are as subject to the 'laws' of nature as any bird, but that belief does not mean the kinds of consequences that other animal species cannot escape will pass us by and leave us unaffected.

Some years ago, W. I. Thomas and Dorothy Swain Thomas made the classic statement that when cultures define something as real, the act has real consequences, regardless of whether it is actually true. But we also need to consider Robert K. Merton's corollary that what is real has consequences whether we define it as real or not.[3]

Having a set of cultural beliefs allows us to live with a taken-for-granted sense of how things are and to treat the 'facts' of our existence as obvious. What we call 'obvious,' however, is not necessarily what is true. It is only assumed to be true beyond doubt in a particular culture. Without a sense of the obvious, social life loses its predictability, and we lose our basis for feeling secure, but the obvious also blinds us to the possibility that what is 'obviously' true may be false.

In this sense, when I hear people accuse sociologists of focusing on the obvious, I feel moved to thank them for their recognition and support, because *someone* should be paying attention to what we all go around assuming to be true. What we do not know often gets us into trouble, but what is right under our noses—including what we *think* we know but don't—can be even more serious. We feel invested in its being true and defend it rather than asking whether we might have it wrong.

U.S. culture, for example, takes it to be obvious that the country is a political democracy and that capitalist 'free enterprise' is democracy's economic equivalent. These beliefs are so powerful that no politician would dare say otherwise, knowing it would be political suicide even to suggest that something might be basically wrong with capitalism. No politician could hope to be elected after pointing out that, in practice, capitalism is anything but democratic, since it concentrates economic power in so few hands that enterprise is 'free' primarily, if not only, for them.[4] The politician would be attacked as disloyal, if not a heretical socialist or communist, for questioning basic beliefs and sacred institutions. And the attacks would come most prominently from the mass media, corporate leaders, privately funded think tanks, and other politicians and government officials, all of whom have a substantial interest in preserving the status quo (including the lopsided distribution of power and wealth), because any challenge to the status quo would antagonize the upper classes on whom they depend. This held true even after the catastrophic financial meltdown of 2008 revealed the extent of reckless misconduct and illegal activity by senior managers in the financial industry.

If the beliefs that identify democracy with capitalism are false or merely hide the truth that underlies the problems that plague us, then the almost-sacred protected status of 'the obvious' becomes a trap, with us right in the middle.

Values, Choice, and Conflict

In a sense, every cultural idea rests on a belief of some kind, because to think about something we first have to see it as something that exists, even if only in our imaginations. But many cultural ideas go beyond basic questions of fact to construct a more complex social reality. Cultural values do this by ranking things in terms of how socially desirable they are—how good or bad, better or worse, superior or inferior they are judged to be.[5]

In many cultures, for example, education is valued above ignorance; honesty above dishonesty; profit above loss; kindness above cruelty; cleanliness above filth; married above single; sex above celibacy; rich above poor; heterosexual above gay, lesbian, or bisexual; white above color; male above female; and being in control above not being in control. In each case, cultural beliefs define what is being compared and ranked. We have to know what we mean by 'education' or who qualifies as 'white' or 'heterosexual,' and beliefs provide the answer. Values take this a step further with a rough hierarchical order that gives various aspects of social life a vertical dimension. In other words, it is not just that 'heterosexual' and 'lesbian' differ in what we think they *are*, for cultural values also rank one as preferable to the other.

Values loom large in our lives because they provide a way to choose between alternatives that might otherwise appear equivalent. Almost everything we do involves a choice among different values, although the choice may come to us so easily that we are not aware of it as such. We decide which clothes to wear each day (or whether to wear them at all); whether to work longer hours to earn more money or fewer hours to spend more time doing other things; whether to get a job right after high school or to go on to college; whether to have sex with someone we feel attracted to; whether to object when we hear sexist, racist, and other forms of oppressive talk; whether to spend the evening reading or watching a movie or surfing the Internet; whether to tell friends about our sexual orientation or keep it to ourselves; whether to vote and for whom; whether to have an abortion or bear a child; or whether to tell friends a truth they would rather not hear. From trivial matters to decisions that can transform our lives or the life of a nation, we are always weighing the relative value of what we see as our alternatives, and cultural values shape how we go about it.

Values do more than influence how we choose between one course of action and another, for they also affect how we perceive and treat ourselves and other people. When values rank European above Latin American, for example, or male above female, or not having a disability above having one, people are sorted into different places in a social hierarchy of worth. This process makes such problems as privilege and oppression more than issues of seeing differences among people. It also ranks entire categories of people in ways that exclude, devalue, and oppress some and include, elevate, and privilege others. The effects of such ranking can be as monumental as the genocidal wars of ethnic cleansing in Rwanda, Darfur, or Bosnia or as subtle as a white waiter's seating a black customer next to the kitchen door and never coming back to take an order. But in every case, what is at stake are the dignity and worth of human beings and the cultural justification of systemic patterns of privilege and oppression.

Like other aspects of culture, values tend to have a taken-for-granted quality about them. We experience them as a natural part of reality, not as socially constructed ideas *about* reality. Our preference for what we value feels so immediate and comes so easily that we assume our particular values are a universal part of the human experience, that there was not a time or a place when people did not feel this way. For some preferences, this is probably true. Even infants would rather be warm than cold, comfortable than in pain, fed rather than hungry.

But most of what we value is what we *learn* to value through socialization in a particular system's culture. A powerful way to see this is to experience cultures that promote different values than our own. A few years ago, for example, I traveled to Norway to visit relatives. We spent several days in the city of Oslo, where the extensive train system runs within the city and outward toward surrounding communities. I was startled to notice trains without conductors to collect fares or punch tickets and train and subway stations with no ways to make sure people paid their fares—no gates, no turnstiles, no ticket booths. I watched people board the train, take out a multiple-ride ticket, and insert it in a machine that punched it each time they rode the train. And I saw people buy single-ride tickets from machines on station platforms and then put the tickets in their pockets since there was no one to collect them.

I cannot imagine U.S. transportation systems operating in this way, and the reason is that the two societies have such different cultures. Norwegian culture includes beliefs that the train system essentially belongs to everyone, that it cannot keep running if people do not pay the fare, and that most people will therefore pay as part of doing their share. The culture also places a higher value on trust than it does on making sure that no one gets away without paying. And it places a higher value on a sense of belonging to the community and doing your bit to make it work than it does on getting something for nothing.

In the United States, however, the belief is that most people will not pay for what they can get for nothing and that getting something for nothing is more important than fostering a sense of community and shared purpose. There are exceptions, especially in smaller communities. In the small town where I live, for example, it is common in the summer to see roadside stands with fruits and vegetables for sale and no one there collecting money, just an open cash box and a sign listing prices. And some colleges have student honor codes instead of exam proctors and other kinds of policing to prevent student cheating. In both cases, a value choice is being made regarding how to organize the system. I am sure that some people take vegetables without paying and that some students cheat and get away with it, and these behaviors violate some important values. But something regarded as even more valuable is gained in this type of system, for people are able to live and work in an atmosphere of mutual trust and respect that is hard to maintain if we are always assuming that everyone will cheat whenever they get the chance.

The more I see of other cultures, the more aware I am of my own culture *as* a culture, and the more I see that things are not just what they *are* but are what my culture makes them out to be. I can also see that when I make choices, I always choose from a limited range of alternatives offered by my culture. This suggests that we never truly make anything like a 'free' choice. As philosopher Arthur Schopenhauer puts it, when it comes to values, "We want what we will, but we don't will what we want."[6]

In other words, when I feel myself wanting a new car, I don't realize how my wanting a new car is connected to a cultural value placed on material possessions—more stuff is better than less, and new stuff is better than old, and stuff I don't have is better than stuff I do. Since we are socialized into a set of cultural values and do not choose how that happens, the values we acquire limit us in ways that are hard to see until we step outside and realize they are not all that's possible.

In that sense, my 'freedom' to want a car is shaped by an economic system that depends on ever-expanding markets and rising profits, both of which depend on encouraging people to measure their lives more by the products and services they consume than, say, by spiritual enlightenment or helping people less well-off than they are, thus setting us up to see the accumulation of material wealth as an essential part of a happy and successful life. This is true of just about everything we value. Whether it's using plastic surgery to 'improve' how we look, aspiring to a college education, not objecting to racist comments as a way to fit in, or seeing our country as superior to all others, we rarely realize how much our culture limits our preferences to a narrow range of possibilities. And we also do not realize how radically different our options might be somewhere else.

As an individual, I can be aware that culture exists and shapes my perceptions and experience, including what I think I want. As someone born and raised in the United States, I can see how materialistic my culture is and choose to live my life differently by pursuing other values. But I will always be doing this *in spite* of my cultural background, as an act of going against what I was raised to value as a path of least resistance. I can expand my freedom only by liberating myself from the narrow range of choices that my culture—that any culture—offers the people who participate in it. To do this, I need to step outside the cultural framework I am used to so that I can see it *as* a framework, as one possibility among many. Stepping outside is an important part of what sociological practice is about, and such concepts as culture, beliefs, and values are important tools used in the process, for they point to what we are stepping outside *of*.

We can go against our culture, because cultures are not rigid frameworks that determine who we are and what we do. Values cannot tell us what to do in every possible situation, because most situations involve combinations of values that are impossible to predict. Instead of giving us clear rules for how to choose in every situation, values provide general guidelines for how to weigh one alternative against another. As social psychologist Roger Brown puts it, values are like rules of grammar that we use to interpret sentences that we've never seen before.[7]

How we apply those rules, however, is up to us. It is generally regarded as good, for example, to choose honesty over dishonesty. But what happens when that value conflicts with another, such as love of family? If murderers come looking for my brother and ask me where he is, you can be sure that I'll do what I can to send them in the wrong direction. But what if my brother is the murderer? What if I'm in the position of David Kaczynski, who realized that his brother, Theodore, might be the Unabomber, whose package bombs killed several people and severely injured numerous others between 1978 and 1995? Do I turn him in for almost certain imprisonment or death, or do I choose loyalty to kin as a higher value and remain silent?

There is no book of answers to such questions, which makes value conflict an enduring source of struggle and anguish. The issue comes up over and over again, whether about protecting the environment at the expense of jobs, making birth control and sex education available in schools, providing a pathway to citizenship for undocumented immigrants, or controlling access to guns. Values provide us with raw materials and rough guidelines for weighing alternatives, but they cannot tell us how to use them.

As part of any culture, values underlie the paths of least resistance that shape how people participate in systems. As a way to regulate people's behavior, however, values can suggest only how we *ought* to behave. What they lack is something to back them up and turn them into statements about how we *must* behave *or else*. Adding the 'or else' to a value gives us something stronger—a norm.

Norms, Morality, and Deviance

The difference between what is valued and desired and what is expected and required is a social consequence in the form of a reward or punishment. If you take a cultural value and turn it into a rule enforced with rewards and punishments, then you have a norm, a value with teeth that can bite if you don't choose the path of least resistance it prescribes.

When David Kaczynski considered whether to turn in his brother to the police, he had to do more than weigh competing values. He also had to consider his behavior in relation to norms and the consequences that go with them. On the one hand, if he turned his brother in, he would be rewarded by a grateful public for ending a nightmare of violence against innocent people. At the same time, he might be punished by family members for violating family norms based on loyalty to kin. On the other hand, if he remained silent, he risked being shamed by a public outraged at his disregard for future victims of his brother's violence. His family, however, might reward him for his loyalty to kin. In either case, his dilemma wasn't simply about choosing between more- or less-valued alternatives. He faced real social consequences no matter what he chose to do.

Notice how changing the system he participated in could change the social consequences of his actions. If his family were formed around both kinship *and* organized crime activities, then his situation might look quite different. Instead of choosing between his duty to society and loyalty to his brother, he would also have to consider what would happen if turning in his brother caused the police to take a close look at his family. To avoid that, he might turn his brother in not to the police but to his family, who might then deal with his brother in its own way to protect the family's 'business' interests.

Like every aspect of culture, norms are made up. They are not what people do but ideas *about* what people do. Like beliefs, norms refer to some aspect of reality, such as the definition of murder. Like values, norms are linked to cultural judgments about what is considered more or less desirable: murder is bad, but killing to protect your country is good. Norms go a step further, however, by linking beliefs and values to social consequences that would not otherwise happen. If a man sets off a bomb near a crowd of people, as at the Boston Marathon in 2013, the result will be injury or death. Whether he'll be arrested, however, and what will happen to him then, depend on what the norms look like, and these can be changed any time a lawmaking body decides. If he is punished, it will not be simply because he has hurt or killed people. It will be because he has violated a norm that prohibits such killing.

To see the difference, consider how he might use a bomb to kill people with different consequences. If he flies a bomber during wartime, for example, or controls a drone flying over Pakistan, he will be rewarded for accomplishing his mission, especially if he is courageous in doing so. The *objective* consequences might be the same—a bomb explodes and kills people, including children and innocent adults—but the social consequences depend on the norms that apply in that system. If a pilot's plane is shot down after he drops the bomb, he might be prosecuted as a criminal by his captors if *their* norms define the killing as an act of murder. In short, we cannot tell what the social consequences of an action will be unless we understand the social system in which it takes place.

Norms are ideas about not only how people behave but also how they appear and, in some cases, who they are. If you walk naked down Main Street at noon on a cold January day, the objective consequence might be that you'll catch a cold or people will see what your body looks like. The social consequences, however, will most likely be something more—from receiving disapproving looks to being arrested. In a nudist colony, however, the social consequence would be acceptance, and disapproving looks would be reserved for people who walked around *without* taking off their clothes.

Norms about personal appearance can be so powerful that we feel bound by them even when we are by ourselves. I was once camping by a lake in a remote section of Vermont, for example, when I decided to go for a swim. I was standing in a beautiful grove of birch trees with no one but my wife for miles around, taking off my clothes and about to put on a bathing suit. Suddenly, with one foot in and one foot out, I was stopped by a question that popped into my mind: why am I putting this suit on? Unable to think of a good reason, I took a wonderful skinny dip, temporarily beyond the reach of cultural norms.

At such moments, we may wonder why norms exist in the first place. Why should anyone care whether we wear clothes at all or clothes that are considered 'appropriate' for the occasion? Why should such rules matter so much that people might be ridiculed, shunned, or even arrested and locked up for breaking them? For that matter, why should we feel justified in shooting someone who is running off with a computer that we consider to be our 'property'? The answer lies in deeper questions of what social systems are about, which, like most important questions, have more than one answer.

One answer comes from what is known as the functional perspective, which is based on the idea that every social system has certain requirements that must be met for it to work. From this perspective, norms exist because without them, systems would fall apart or foul up in one way or another. This makes sense, given that social systems are organized around relationships among people, and relationships consist largely of what we expect of one another. Since norms define and enforce expectations, it follows that a social system cannot do without them.

Norms also play an important part in defining a system's boundaries by giving us a way to tell insiders from outsiders and by controlling who gets to be one or the other. To belong to a community, for example, you have to go along with its culture to a certain degree, and you can often tell members from nonmembers by who does and who does not. If you break the rules, you risk punishment, including being thrown out altogether. This is not just because you have violated a norm but because the norms are connected to beliefs and values that define reality and what is considered important. The surest way to gain acceptance and influence in a group is to adopt its culture openly and from the outset. Rejecting a culture is the surest way to be rejected yourself, no matter what you might have to contribute.

This is why when new students flood a college campus in the fall, they wander around looking lost—they *are* lost, and this makes it easy to pick them out from a crowd. They break rules left and right because they don't know the rules even exist, and so they may be forgiven for a while. But there comes a point when they are expected to know what is what and are held accountable for what they do as the price of being included. They have crossed a boundary defined in part by their relationship to a set of cultural ideas about who they are in relation to something larger than themselves.

In this sense, it doesn't matter what the norms actually are in a social system, so long as there are some. When children create a club, for example, one of the first things they do is make up rules that have to be obeyed to belong. To have a club without rules is unthinkable, no matter how silly or contradictory they may be. The rules themselves do not matter as much as establishing a sense of something larger that members can feel part of, which, in turn, also tells them something about who they are.

The great French sociologist Émile Durkheim sees this collective sense of 'we' as the necessary foundation of social life and the only way to control people's behavior.[8] This collective sense is what morality is really all about—not just a set of rules about how to be a good person, but a shared sense of what the essence of a social system and its people consists of. It is from that shared sense of 'us' and 'it' that morality draws much of its power and authority, for to violate moral rules is to risk our sense of belonging to the system itself—the family, the community, the society. From Durkheim's sociological perspective, the most important thing about morality is not behavior but the feeling of attachment that binds people to a group, community, or society when they support its moral rules. Without this, people feel lost, and systems can fall apart.

From this perspective, when people break a rule, they do much more than that, for they also violate a sense of boundaries and raise questions about who they are in relation to an entire system. If you wear the 'wrong' clothes to work, people start wondering whether you really belong there, whether you're really committed to what the place is 'all about.' You might think, "What's a dress code got to do with morality?" In the usual sense of what makes a good person, the answer is probably "Not much" in most systems most of the time. But in a larger sociological sense, morality is a basis for defining what a group or society *is* and what it takes to be accepted as a member. This makes the answer more complex. Whether it is rules about killing people or how to behave at the dinner table, *all* norms have some bearing on belonging and commitment that can tell us as much about ourselves as about the systems we participate in.

If morality is basically about belonging, then it follows that people who are seen as outsiders will be treated as deviants, violators of a moral code. This is what happens when people are stigmatized, treated as deviant not because of something they have done but because of who they are.[9] This often plays a key role in various forms of social inequality and oppression. In many ways, such characteristics as race, gender, ethnicity, sexual orientation, disability status, and religion are often used to define deviant categories of people who are then treated as outsiders by dominant groups. They are denied the normal, everyday benefits of belonging, from being treated with courtesy and respect in a store to being able to find a place to live, walk safely down the street, or get a job that reflects their abilities.

For centuries, for example, women have been regarded as deviants—as incomplete, flawed versions of men, whose minds and bodies render them weak and not up to the standards of a fully developed and competent human being.[10] In most valued occupations and professions, women may still find themselves treated as outsiders and be told in ways both subtle and overt that they have no right to be there and are unwelcome. Whether a woman is not invited to join a group of men going out for a beer after work or finds a used condom in her desk drawer and suffers other forms of harassment, the underlying message and its effect are the same.[11]

The use of norms to exclude and oppress entire categories of people suggests something going on that a functionalist perspective does not help us see. It makes sense that systems are organized in ways that regulate what people *do*, but it makes much less sense to argue for some kind of social need to regulate who people *are* in terms of such traits as the color of their skin or whether they identify as gay or straight. It is hard to see why a society would require arrangements that not only elevate and privilege some groups but also routinely inflict suffering on everyone else.

Systematic patterns of exclusion, exploitation, domination, and abuse make more sense from what is known in sociological practice as 'the conflict perspective.' The conflict perspective also focuses on systems but primarily as a setting for conflict around patterns of social inequality. Culture is where we get most of the ideas we use to define reality, to differentiate superior from inferior, and to identify the rules of social life. It is therefore not surprising that privileged groups use their power and influence to shape culture in their own interests, including the perpetuation of privilege.

Consider, for example, cultural ideas about private property. The idea of property has not been around for very long, dating back no more than several thousand years. For something to be regarded as property, it has to occupy a particular position in a social relationship. When I say that the land my house sits on is my property, I'm saying that the people of my community and society recognize my right to live on it and do pretty much what I want with it, although not without limits. This allows me some control over who comes onto the property and how they treat it. With few exceptions, my property cannot be changed, destroyed, or taken away from me without my consent, unless it's done by a nonhuman force, such as an earthquake. In this sense, property is not some*thing* (or, in the case of people held in slavery, some*one*). Instead, property is a set of *ideas* about the relationships that connect 'owners' to what is socially *regarded* as their property and to other people and social systems, such as communities and societies.

What we call 'property' exists only when cultures have beliefs that define it as real. Like many Native American tribes, for example, the Wampanoag traditionally viewed land as part of nature and not something that people could own. They could live on it, farm it, hunt on it, worship it, and admire its beauty, but they could not treat it as property. When English settlers came to the island of Nantucket off the southern coast of Massachusetts, however, and 'purchased' land from the tribe, the Wampanoag believed they had sold the English only a right to share in use of the land. They were dumbfounded, then, by what the white settlers did next: the English arrested and punished anyone who 'trespassed' on what they now regarded as 'private property.' The Wampanoag could no longer walk on or otherwise use the land, because it no longer 'belonged' to them. The Wampanoag social system had no place for such ideas. To the Wampanoag, the norms of English culture defined a relationship to the land that simply was not possible.[12]

In theory, norms that protect private property serve the interests of everyone who has any, whether it's my iPad or Exxon's oil wells. And the more property you own, the more you benefit from those norms. But protection takes on greater significance when property is a basis for systems of privilege and oppression. When owning property gives people power over others, then any norm that protects property rights also protects the inequality of power and privilege and what people are able to do with it.

In the United States, for example, a tiny portion of the population owns or controls the vast majority of wealth, especially the factories, machinery, tools, and other resources that people use to produce wealth and to make a living. The wealthiest 20 percent of U.S. families own almost 90 percent of all the wealth, the top 10 percent own 73 percent, and the wealthiest 1 percent own 35 percent. By comparison, the bottom 40 percent own 0.2 percent. Across the world as a whole, the pattern is much the same, with the top 20 percent owning 85 percent of all wealth and the bottom 50 percent owning barely 1 percent.[13]

A lopsided distribution of wealth does not mean that norms protecting private property exist only for the elite who own most of it. It does mean, however, that while the law protects everyone's property, it also enables the elite to maintain its privileged position, including its ability to increase its share of wealth even further. If you own or control businesses and factories, you can decide who works and who does not, how they work, and what becomes of the goods and services they produce. You can decide whether to close up shop and move production and jobs to another region or country where labor costs are lower, environmental and worker safety laws and labor unions are weaker, and profit margins are therefore higher. You can tell communities and states that unless they give your company tax breaks, you will move to a 'friendlier' business climate. And when states and communities agree to such demands rather than see jobs go elsewhere, people who live and work in these areas have to make up the lost taxes or make do with less money for schools and other government services.

Seeing how different aspects of social life fit together is an important part of sociological practice, for everything in social life is connected to something else. Notice, for example, that a culture cannot include values and norms about property unless it also has a cultural belief that defines such a thing as property as real in the first place. Notice also that norms that seem to support one value are likely to affect other values as well, so that what appears to be just about protecting property can also be about preserving an entire social order based on privilege and oppression.

Such patterns of interconnection appear in every aspect of social life: the connections that we see right away and most easily are usually just the tip of the iceberg. In this way, sociological practice can take us beneath the surface toward the deeper truth of what is going on, why it matters, and what it has to do with us.

Attitudes: Culture as Feeling

Beliefs, values, and norms have a huge influence on how we perceive reality, how we think about it, and how we behave. If we look at heterosexist prejudice, for example, we can see how elements of all three kinds of ideas combine. Prejudice against gay, lesbian, and bisexual people values one sexual orientation above all others. The values are typically propped up by beliefs that define sexual orientation as a type of person and make heterosexuals look better. Heterosexuality, for example, may be seen as natural and healthy, while anything else is seen as unnatural, a disease or perversion, or an offense against God.

Since heterosexism elevates one sexual orientation above others, it becomes a form of privilege in that heterosexuals are treated better simply because of their sexual orientation. Like all forms of privilege, heterosexual privilege is supported and maintained by norms that in various ways keep lesbian, gay, and bisexual people in their place by discriminating against them in such areas as housing, work, and parental and spousal rights. A lesbian couple might live together and share their lives for twenty years, yet if one becomes seriously ill, her parents and not her life partner are likely to be the ones legally recognized as having the right to manage her care and finances if she cannot manage them for herself.[14]

As powerful as beliefs, values, and norms are, they do not account for the feelings involved in prejudice. Hatred, disgust, or fear directed at gays, lesbians, and bisexuals, for example, is not a belief, a value, or a norm, even though such emotions may be closely connected to cultural ideas. Straight men may feel contempt for gay men and connect that feeling to beliefs and values that render gays contemptible in straight men's eyes. And they may express their contempt through norms that disadvantage and oppress gays. In both cases, the contempt is more than a feeling. It is also a cultural attitude that blends belief, value, and emotion in ways that shape how we feel and behave toward people or, for that matter, the Earth, ideas, or just about anything else.[15] The feelings can be as intense and momentous as unbridled public hatred. Or they can be subtle and everyday, in the hidden sense of unease that straight men often feel when they are around gay men.[16]

In each case, the feeling is more than an emotion, for it is rooted in a social system and a culture that goes with it. Feelings depend on how people define the reality of what is going on, what matters most, and what is expected of them and regarded as socially appropriate. Whether they take the form of the most intense heterosexist hatred in a violent crime against gays or the most restrained politeness at the dinner table, attitudes are a complex blend of ideas and feelings that shape how people participate in social life.

Some emotions are probably hardwired into us as a species. Small children, for example, do not have to be taught to feel afraid. Fear is certainly an emotion, but it's not a cultural attitude unless it is connected to beliefs or values. Some years ago, for example, my wife wanted to expand our household by adding a snake to our two dogs and two goats. When I first heard the suggestion, I reacted as most people in this society would: "You want a *what?*"

Eventually, however, I was persuaded to consider that there was no reason to feel afraid or disgusted other than what I'd learned from cultural attitudes about snakes. I went, I saw, I touched, and I discovered much to my surprise that this creature was, in fact, a gentle being with skin that felt like fine leather. Perhaps most importantly, I realized that for all my bad feelings about snakes, this animal—Oya is her name—had far more to fear from me than I from her. She can barely hear or see and explores her environment primarily by smelling with her tongue. I could kill her whenever I wanted, and she would barely see it coming. Oya, however, would never strike at me unless she felt threatened and, even then, could not hurt me very much unless she got lucky. When I tell this story, people almost always react with a mixture of disgust and fear, even though only a few of them have been close enough to snakes to hold them or look in their faces. Their fear is less about actual experience than about growing up and living in a social system whose culture is full of frightening images of snakes.

In one sense, then, attitudes can be primary emotions, such as fear, that are attached to various cultural beliefs and values. By itself, fear is not an attitude, but a cultural fear of snakes is. Many attitudes, however, are emotions that exist only in relation to a social context. Contempt and disgust, for example, exist only as expressions of negative judgments, and you cannot judge something without using beliefs and values. You can teach infants to fear just about anything—a banana, a person—just by pairing it with something inherently fearful, such as violence or sudden loud noises. But you cannot teach infants to feel disgust for something, because they have no way to form ideas and judgments about anything until they learn to use language.

Put something delicious in a baby's mouth, for example, and it'll be gone in no time. But put the same thing in my mouth and tell me that it's dog meat (a delicacy in many parts of Asia), and it won't stay in my mouth for long. My reaction of disgust won't be because of the taste but because of cultural ideas about what I think I'm eating. Give a juicy hamburger to someone who enjoys eating meat and, when they're halfway through eating it, say that it's made of ground cat and watch how they react to see the power of cultural attitudes in action. Even if you then tell them that it's not really cat, they may still refuse to eat it.

The mix of emotions, beliefs, and values is at the core of what makes a cultural attitude. Pride, shame, guilt, love, hate, loyalty, reverence, respect, disrespect, haughtiness, humility, pity, patriotism, sympathy, empathy, gratitude, arrogance—all exist only in relation to ideas about the object of the feeling. This is also true of what is often thought to be an absence of emotion, as in attitudes of detachment or emotional deadness. In this sense, there is no such thing as being 'unemotional,' because 'unfeeling' is as much an emotional state as 'deeply moved' or 'enraged.' Very often, when people say they don't feel anything, they are experiencing a kind of flat emptiness that is very much an emotional state, even though they may not call it that. And it is a feeling that can shape how they behave in powerful ways. It can mask and underlie great cruelty, for example, or make it easier for people to kill thousands in warfare, to do things that might sicken and horrify them if they allowed themselves to feel *those* feelings instead of the feeling of flat, detached I'm-just-doing-my-job efficiency that often takes their place.

Although we do not think of it as such in this culture, 'unemotional' is a powerful attitude that is especially expected of men and, not surprisingly, those in positions of power. The only emotion that is routinely allowed and encouraged in men is anger, because anger, like emotional detachment, makes it easier to exercise power and control. Since many cultures link standards for manhood and leadership to men's ability to keep themselves in a seemingly unemotional state, anyone who aspires to those positions will feel compelled to adopt that attitude. The attitude combines a feeling of emotional detachment with cultural beliefs about the consequences of allowing various kinds of emotions to influence judgments and decisions. It is also connected to values that rank stereotypical masculine inexpressiveness above the stereotypical feminine tendency to be openly 'emotional.' As a result, women, who are culturally encouraged to be 'emotional,' will be encouraged to cultivate an 'unemotional' attitude if they want to be taken seriously and succeed in the male-dominated business and professional world.

This dynamic happens with many forms of social inequality—those in lower positions are often culturally stereotyped as more emotional than those in higher positions, and this perception can easily be used against them. When black people or women express anger at discrimination in the workplace, for example, they risk triggering stereotypes of black people and women as overly emotional and therefore out of control and needing to be controlled by others. This, in turn, is used to argue that they are unsuited for higher positions, because they do not display appropriate attitudes.

Looking at attitudes and how they work is a useful way to see how various aspects of culture combine to produce complex and powerful results. Although culture consists primarily of what we cannot see—symbols, ideas, and feelings—it also includes the material world that humans construct as part of their social environment.

Material Culture and the Stuff of Life

The reality we construct is both nonmaterial and material. For example, we can think of music as a form of culture, as patterns of sound that we recognize as music rather than noise. In many cultures, music is expressed in a symbolic form using notes, sharps, flats, rests, and the like that musicians must know to 'read' what other musicians write (although one can play music without being able to read it). But as a part of culture, music also has a material basis for its existence, from the paper it is printed on to the brass, wood, steel, animal skins, bones, shells, and other materials that go into making instruments. In industrial societies, the hardware for producing and reproducing music seems to expand daily, from microphones and mixers to electric violins, synthesizers, and MP3 players.

What all this means for sociological practice is that to understand music or any other part of social life, we have to pay attention to its material *and* nonmaterial aspects and how they are related to one another. The terms of social life are not simply embodied in who we are as people but also embodied in how we shape the physical world, from the furniture we sit on to the cities and towns we live in.

Material culture exists because human beings seem to have an inherent tendency to transform the world as we find it. Whether it is to cut a path through the woods from the village to the water source, plant a garden, lay down a highway, build a house, or turn iron ore into steel, we seem bent toward the creative work of turning one thing into something else.

How we do this matters on several levels. In the most immediate sense, the material world we create directly affects our own physical existence. The telephone, for example, takes our limited ability to hear and extends it across thousands of miles. In the opposite direction, the walls of buildings—especially windowless ones in buildings where many people work—can shut us in and close us off from the world around us and the people in it. By itself, the human body cannot do very much. Our senses of smell, sight, hearing, taste, and touch do not measure up very well compared with those of many species. We cannot fly, and most mammals can outrun or outswim us without too much trouble. In the overall scheme of things, in short, we're an awkward and limited bunch.

But our ability to invent material culture more than makes up for these limitations, which is a blessing and a curse. The blessing is that we can do creative things that are otherwise far beyond our reach. The curse is that we can use material culture to do damage beyond our wildest imaginings. The human ability to pollute and otherwise destroy the life-sustaining capacity of the planet is so vast and complex that we are only beginning to grasp the scope of it. And our ability to use technology not only to eradicate entire species whose presence we find objectionable but also to slaughter other human beings in huge numbers continues to increase, with no apparent end in sight.

Beyond our physical existence, material culture also affects the terms on which social life is lived. It affects how we perceive reality, how we feel, what we value and expect from other people, and how social relationships are structured around such issues as the distribution of power. When Johannes Gutenberg invented movable type in the fifteenth century, for example, he helped bring about a social revolution. For the first time, it was possible to take information or an idea, reproduce it in written form, and distribute it to a huge audience. This meant that it now mattered whether most people could read and write, because when books were created by hand, only the wealthy could afford them. As literacy spread, ideas, information, innovation, and invention spread right along with it.

In the simplest sense, a printing press is just a machine, a collection of parts arranged in a certain way. Its social significance comes from how it has been used, especially in choosing what to print. Since what people read influences how they perceive and think about the world, it was inevitable that groups would struggle to control the printing press as a way to control the flow of information and ideas. At one time or another, just about every government in the world has tried to limit people's access to printing presses and related technology and what they print on them. In the 1980s, the Romanian government went so far as to require people who owned typewriters to register them with the police so that the authorities could use samples of their type to identify the origin of antigovernment writing. If you had a criminal record or were seen as someone who posed "a danger to public order and security," you could not own a typewriter at all.[17]

In less-authoritarian societies, the state has less control over printing and publishing. This doesn't mean that most people have access to this material culture, however, because it is quite expensive. As a result, writes Michael Parenti, freedom of the press exists primarily for those who own the presses or have the money to buy space in newspapers and magazines and print what they want to say.[18] Increasingly, the public flow of ideas and information is controlled by a shrinking number of corporations that expand by merging and buying one another. This is happening across all areas of mass media, from television, radio, and film to books, magazines, and newspapers. The rate of acquisitions and mergers and the consolidation of power and control is so rapid that it's difficult to keep up with who owns whom. It is hard to find a major book publisher, for example, that isn't owned by another company, sometimes a still-larger publisher but increasingly a corporation that otherwise has nothing to do with publishing.

Why does this consolidation in the flow of ideas and information matter? It matters because what can appear to be a diversity of independent news, information, and analysis can, in fact, flow from a small number of sources whose interests take first priority. As one commentator responds to a series of acquisitions and mergers (which have since undoubtedly been superseded by still more shuffling of ownership, power, and control):

> Watch a Little, Brown book become a Book of the Month Club pick, a Warner paperback and a Warner Brothers film that is featured in *People*, reviewed in *Time*, with a soundtrack album on Atlantic Records, shown on *HBO*, parodied in *Mad* and finally developed into a TV series by Lorimar. And all of the money—along with all of the choices—will be left in the hands of Time Warner, Inc.[19]

What looks like a free and open marketplace of ideas turns out to be something else altogether (although it remains to be seen how this consolidation of power will be affected by the increasing use of the Internet and social media to provide information and analysis). The situation has been even more extreme since the 2010 *Citizens United v. Federal Election Commission* case, in which the U.S. Supreme Court ruled that corporations are 'persons' under the Constitution and entitled to contribute as much money as they want to political campaigns.[20]

Social control over the flow of ideas would be an issue even without the trend toward consolidating power in mass media. Almost none of the media, for example, has anything serious to say about capitalism and how it affects most people's lives. If you want to learn more about this, you won't find it on television or the radio, even on the supposedly liberal-biased public networks. Nor will you find it in newspapers, news magazines, or the lists of major book publishers. Why not? It could be that there isn't anything critical to say because capitalism is so close to perfection that, aside from minor flaws, it's as good as an economic system can get. Given the amount of suffering and crisis that has become almost routine in the world, however, it is unlikely that we've arrived at such a happy state.

It is more likely that the mass media are silent on the subject of capitalism because they are organized in ways that make silence a path of least resistance. For example, almost all of the mass media are capitalist corporations. As such, they are owned by stockholders looking for the highest return on their investment and controlled by executives whose fortunes depend on how well they serve stockholder interests. In other words, those who own and control the mass media have a vested financial and power interest in preserving and promoting capitalism as an economic system. They have little to gain and a lot to lose by suggesting there might be something wrong with it. This makes them unlikely to question or undermine the system that makes their power and privilege possible.

None of this means that the mass media control what we think about a particular issue, but they do have a great deal of control over what issues we think *about*. And if they can control *whether* we see something like capitalism as an issue, they do not have to worry about *how* we see it as an issue. In this sense, the most profound use of media power is not in what is printed, filmed, or broadcast but in what is *not*. It's no wonder that even as major social problems, such as privilege and oppression and chronic economic insecurity, affect more and more people, it does not occur to the media to ask how a system as powerful and pervasive as capitalism might be part of the problem. This silence is what made the Occupy Wall Street movement so unusual when it emerged in 2011, challenging not only capitalism but also the power of corporations to influence government for their own gain at the public expense, even to the extent of violating laws without being prosecuted.

Clearly the problem has less to do with the existence of material culture, such as the printing press or television camera or Internet server, than it does with how this culture is used in a particular system. If we overlook the difference between the thing and how it's used, material culture can take on a life of its own, as if it has power over us all by itself. Computers, for example, take a lot of blame for supposedly controlling people's lives, but the problem is not the machine. The problem is in our relationship to the machine and how we think about it, both of which we control more than we know. A computer is, after all, just metal and plastic and amounts to nothing more than that unless someone plugs it in, turns it on, and tells it what to do. As such, a computer is nothing more than what we make it to be and has no more significance than we choose to give it. In the early stages of the Industrial Revolution in Europe, for example, workers saw machines as evil because machines were being used to replace and control workers. The words 'saboteur' and 'sabotage,' in fact, come from the practice of taking wooden-soled shoes—*sabots*—and throwing them in the works to disable or ruin the hated machines.

Today, the use of machines to replace and control workers is expanding rapidly, primarily in the form of computers and robotics. Nothing about the machinery itself, however, requires this to happen. More efficient production could be used to reduce the number of hours people work and still provide enough goods and services to meet everyone's needs. In a capitalist economic system, however, this is not what 'efficient' means. A capitalist organization increases efficiency by maximizing production and minimizing cost—especially the cost of labor—which leads to higher profits. So, the 'leisure' that workers gain from the increased use of 'labor-saving' technology tends to be the spare time afforded by unemployment or forced early retirement rather than a full-time job that demands less from them in return for being able to earn a living. Amid a technological explosion, people in the United States are not working less; they are working more, and without much to show for it.[21]

The stuff of material culture cannot tell us what it is about. For that, we have to see where material culture fits in a social system; how people perceive, value, and think about it; and what they do with it. As such, material culture can take social life in many different directions at once. The computer, for example, can be used as an instrument of oppressive control. It can store enormous amounts of personal information about people and be used to invade their privacy and monitor their every movement in the workplace and beyond. In some businesses, workers must use a coded key card to enter or leave any room, including the bathroom. This provides information about where workers are from one moment to the next throughout the day, even at times when you might think it is no one's business but their own. On a larger scale, governments use cell-phone technology to track people's movements and additional technology to monitor e-mail and phone calls on a global scale.

Technology, however, can serve any purpose we can imagine. The Internet, for example, makes it possible for anyone with a computer and an on-line connection to access a worldwide communications system that—so far—is virtually impossible for anyone to control (which hasn't stopped some governments, such as in Egypt and China, from trying). The Internet consists of millions of individual computers connected in small networks that are themselves linked to one another to make larger networks. No one knows from one day to the next how many computers are involved, and certainly no one can know all the billions of possible routes that connect those computers to one another. There are no central switching stations as there are in telephone systems, no centralized control points to shut down or regulate the flow of information. If one computer network isn't working, then information is simply routed to its destination through one of countless other networks. E-mail messages don't even travel in single units but are first broken into 'packets,' which are sent off in different directions and reassembled in their original form at their destination.

It is virtually impossible to control such a decentralized system as a whole, which is why governments interested in controlling the flow of information—which includes most governments—are working hard to invent technology to control cyberspace. And with good reason: in Egypt, for example, the authoritarian regime of Hosni Mubarak was brought down in 2011 by a popular uprising that mobilized protestors largely through the use of the Internet and cell phones.

Although material culture gets relatively little attention in sociological work, it can play a complex and paradoxical role in social life. We create this material culture and make it part of our identities, and yet we often experience it as separate and external—autonomous and powerful in relation to ourselves. We tend to identify with it in the sense that we come to depend on it so heavily that we cannot imagine life without it. At the same time, we can easily forget that it's nothing more than something human beings have made.

The danger of identifying with material culture is that we may hang onto it even when it produces terrible consequences. We think we cannot live without cars, air-conditioning, cell phones, and CO_2-producing power plants, but global warming makes clear that in the long term, we cannot live *with* them.[22] There is also danger in seeing material culture as alien and separate from our ability to create it. It is dangerous because even if we want to change or get rid of it, we may feel helpless or, worse, that it isn't our responsibility in the first place. This is how we can find ourselves feeling and acting as if we are at the mercy of inanimate objects.

It is all too easy to forget that the sum total of any culture is the product of the abundant potential of human imagination. "We live in a web of ideas, a fabric of our own making," writes philosopher Susanne Langer.[23] But as we live inside this web, what it appears to be at the moment is always only part of what is possible. This profoundly limits our ability to grasp the larger sense of what is going on. We live as though we exist inside a little box of reality constructed from cultural stuff—whether in a family, at work, online, or in society at large. And we rarely see beyond it, primarily because we do not even know the box is there. We act as though what we see is simply all there is. But it's not, and to imagine something more, we first have to see it for what it is. In other words, to see *beyond* the box, we first have to take a serious look *at* the box, which is what sociological practice urges us to do.

Our Box, the Best Box, the Only Box

Living inside a box that we can't see out of makes it easy to assume that other cultures either don't exist or, if they do, are either just like ours or not worth the bother of getting to know, a phenomenon known as 'ethnocentrism.' We are like infants who see themselves and their experience as the center of the universe and with no awareness that there might be anything else beyond what we know.

The 'box' goes with us wherever we go, including other societies, which, of course, have cultures of their own. I vividly remember being deep inside Mexico and hearing a U.S. tourist's angry outburst at a restaurant waiter who would not accept dollars as payment for the meal. The tourist could not imagine a place where dollars were not the currency of choice and refused to allow any other possibility. His tone conveyed the unmistakable message that being from the United States gave him a sense of arrogant entitlement, as in "Who are you to refuse my money?" But it also reflected an underlying phenomenon that is nearly universal—the difficulty in seeing beyond our own society.

The tourist's blind arrogance was ethnocentric, but he was also ethnocentric in his assumption that any culture other than his own was inferior. He assumed that U.S. dollars were a superior currency to Mexican pesos and that the waiter should accept, if not be grateful for, an offering of this more-valuable currency. However, at that time the peso had a much more stable history of maintaining its value than did the dollar and, if anything, the U.S. tourist held a less-desirable currency. But in a world seen through ethnocentric eyes, none of that mattered. The tourist resisted anything that might raise questions about the comfortable box he lived in, beginning with awareness of the box itself and even the possibility of something else.

Ethnocentrism is everywhere and not peculiar to any culture. It is what led Europeans to call the Americas 'the New World' and to assume the right to name it, conquer its peoples, and plunder its resources. It is why Columbus Day is celebrated in the United States to recognize the 'discovery' of America, even though North America was discovered many thousands of years before by migrants from Siberia to Alaska. Ethnocentrism explains why white Australians celebrate the 'founding' of Australia in 1788, even though numerous tribal groups trace their lineage back to ancestors living there some forty thousand years before the coming of Europeans. It is why the Japanese first greeted shipwrecked European sailors as 'barbarians' and promptly executed them. And it's why virtually every country that goes to war underestimates the courage, tenacity, and resources of its opponents, often assuming victory will come in a matter of weeks or months, as when the United States invaded Iraq in 2003.

In some ways, a kind of ethnocentrism operates not only among societies but often within them as well. In complex societies, dominant groups often act as though the cultural ideas they use to construct reality apply to everyone. Heterosexuals, for example, act as though they can assume everyone they encounter is also heterosexual and carry on conversations as though that assumption were true. In similar ways, whites, Christians, men, and the middle class often act as though their outlooks and ways of life are at the center of the social universe and represent human experience in general.

Most businesses in the United States, for example, routinely make little or no allowance for holidays not associated with being white, Christian, and of northern European background.[24] This pattern occurs in the larger public world as well. The routine use of the phrase "Have a Merry Christmas" in casual public talk, for example, reflects an assumption that everyone celebrates or values Christmas. Is a Jew, Buddhist, or atheist supposed to smile in return and say, "Thanks! Merry Christmas to you, too"?

In this sense, every complex society includes a wide range of socially constructed realities, but some dominate and come to stand for the whole. The result is a kind of internal ethnocentrism in which diversity and difference are treated as invisible or, when acknowledged at all, as inferior.

The concept of ethnocentrism reveals how every culture limits the view of people who participate in it. But it also points to a basic paradox of culture and how we live and use it. 'Ethnocentrism' is, after all, just a word and as such is a part of culture, the very thing it helps us see more clearly. In this sense, culture can take us in two directions at once. It can take us inward, into the limited space of our particular cultural box. But as tools for sociological practice, such concepts as culture and ethnocentrism also point to the box itself and toward the powerful experience of imagining ourselves inside and outside at the same time.

3

The Structures of Social Life

I was in my second year of graduate school when I made my first trip to San Miguel de Allende, a small town nestled on a mountainside in central Mexico. The trip was the closest I'd come to a real vacation in a long time—weeks with no responsibilities, day after day of long walks, good books to read, sleep whenever I wanted it, and freely taking in the smells, tastes, sights, and sounds of open-air markets, sunbaked adobe, and beautiful gardens.

After several weeks of this, I had a strange experience. For some reason that I no longer recall, I wanted to know what time it was and realized that I had stopped wearing my watch. I knew it was afternoon and not evening, but beyond that, I had no clue. Since I hadn't been doing anything that required me to know the time, I had lost my sense of it. At first, I was fascinated by this experience of being timeless, but then I realized that I also didn't know what day of the week it was, even after I sat for a while trying to figure it out. This was a bit disturbing, as if I were lost, like taking a subway to the usual stop and coming up into a neighborhood I'd never seen before.

In a social sense, 'lost' is what I was. Certain rhythms and cycles in life seem natural and built into our experience as human beings. The passing of the seasons is one, as is the difference between night and day and the circadian rhythms that regulate when we feel drawn to sleep or wakefulness. But knowing the time of day by the clock is not one of them.

them, but it is also true that they exist independently of being occupied by particular people at any given time. The game of Monopoly, for example, exists regardless of whether anyone plays it at the moment. In the same way, the U.S. Supreme Court exists as a system over and above the nine people who currently occupy the status of Justice. If the justices all died in a plane crash, the Court would still exist, even though its key statuses were currently unoccupied.

The distinction between statuses and the people who occupy them is crucial for understanding how social life works. If we confuse the two, it is easy to make the mistake of trying to explain social phenomena solely in terms of individuals. Every time a U.S. president appoints a new Supreme Court justice, for example, there is speculation about how the candidate will vote on controversial issues, such as abortion, same-sex marriage, immigration, or affirmative action. Legal scholars remind us, however, that people's opinions before going on the Court often don't tell us much about how they will vote in their new role. This is because the status of Supreme Court justice places powerful limits on anyone who occupies it, which new justices may not realize until they actually get there. There is a huge burden of responsibility that comes with being one of the nine most powerful judges in the entire country, whose decisions can shape the course of history. This is why the Court places a high value on precedents set by past decisions and strongly discourages overturning them. Technically, justices can vote however they want, but in practice, they rarely feel free to do so, because they feel limited by the responsibilities that go with occupying the status of Supreme Court justice.

This suggests that if we want to know how people will behave, we are in many ways better off knowing the statuses they occupy than their personal characteristics and intentions. When U.S. voters elect a new president, for example, they often look for candidates who can change the direction of government policy, solve social problems, and transform the landscape of social life. Newly elected presidents often take office determined to change how things are done, but they soon realize that although their status is the most powerful in the entire political system, it is just one of many that make that system work the way it does. While the electorate is quick to blame politicians for not delivering on their promises, they forget how much easier it is to put new people into systems than it is to change systems themselves.

When the Bill Clinton administration tried to overhaul the nation's health-insurance system in 1993, for example, it ran into opposition from every side as the complexity of that system and the implications of changing it became apparent. Providing affordable health care for everyone was not simply a matter of what was good for people's health or what the president wanted. It also had to accommodate a complex web of competing interests, including insurance and drug companies, physicians, businesses, labor unions, the elderly, the wealthy, the middle class, and those living in poverty. In the end, it became an exercise in frustration that satisfied no one except, perhaps, those who wanted things to stay as they were. When President Barack Obama took office in 2009, he encountered similar problems enacting a reform program of his own.

Heads of state may be among the most powerful officeholders in the world, but office*holders* are what they are. As such, when people are elected to high office, they do not simply occupy a status. More importantly, the status they occupy is connected to a vast network of statuses within and outside the government, and those *relationships* limit what they can accomplish. The power of leaders to affect so many people is also what limits them, for every move they make produces a complex range of consequences that shape and limit the options from which they choose. No status *simply* empowers—it also constrains, in some ways *more* than it empowers.

What makes things still more complicated is that we participate in a variety of systems, which means we occupy many different statuses. Some statuses are ascribed to us at birth, such as race, gender, ethnicity, and family statuses, such as daughter. Others we achieve and occupy as we move through our lives, such as student, clerk, plumber, lawyer, manager, teacher, soldier, wife, husband, life partner, mother, father, stepparent. Notice that with ascribed and achieved statuses, we occupy the status regardless of whether we're actually *doing* anything related to it. My father, for example, died some years ago, and yet I am still his son. In this sense, we occupy such statuses no matter where we are or whom we're with, and we may be known by them to ourselves and to other people.

There are other statuses that we do not occupy all the time because they exist only in a particular situation. When I step onto a sidewalk, for example, I occupy the status of pedestrian. As soon as I step off the sidewalk and onto a bus, I exit 'pedestrian' and enter 'bus passenger.' With situational statuses, we have to be actively *doing* something to occupy it. Many statuses, then, have to do with *who* and *where* we are in social terms, while others have to do simply with *where* we are and what we're doing at the moment.

The point of occupying a status is that it connects us to social systems and provides us with paths of least resistance that shape how we experience and participate in those systems. It does this with a set of cultural ideas known as a role.[3] A role is a collection of beliefs, values, attitudes, and norms that apply to whoever occupies a particular status in relation to whoever occupies another status in the system. The role of teacher, for example, includes beliefs that describe the kind of person a teacher is supposed to be, such as the knowledge and credentials that people can assume teachers will have. It also includes values that shape a teacher's choices, such as the importance of learning and growth, and norms that regulate how they behave, such as those requiring them to attend faculty meetings or barring them from sexually harassing students. There are also attitudes such as respect for students and taking them seriously.

Notice that the status of teacher comes with several different roles, one for each of the other statuses in the system that are related to it. The teacher's role in relation to students is quite different from the role in relation to other teachers or to the dean or students' parents. In each case, the status remains constant, but the content of the role varies from one relationship to another.

Roles lay out paths of least resistance that shape how we appear and behave in countless ways. In schools and workplaces, for example, there is a lot of pressure to have the answer to every question, which makes always coming up with an answer (whether or not you know what you're talking about) a path of least resistance for people in many different statuses. You could, of course, choose otherwise, by saying, "I don't know," when someone asks a question. But, as an employee of a large corporation once told me, "In this place, it's not okay to say you don't know." The "not okay" points to a form of social resistance—a social consequence—that is built into the system itself through its statuses and roles and discourages people from choosing alternative paths.

Given how many statuses we occupy and all the roles that go with them, social life can get complicated when we're presented with more than one path at once. Such choices create the problem of role conflict, when the ideas of one role conflict with those of another. When male teachers, for example, try to initiate sexual relationships with female students, the result is a role conflict that can severely compromise both roles.[4] For the teacher, it becomes impossible to treat her as he would any other student. For the student, the conflict threatens not only her success within the narrow confines of school but also, especially for graduate students, the course of her entire career and life. If she refuses him, he can use his power to exclude or punish her academically. If she consents, she may benefit from some sort of favoritism for a while but will always be vulnerable to being undone by it. If others find out, she may be denigrated for 'sleeping her way to the top.' Or, he may decide to use the power of his position against her if she displeases him or if he grows tired of her.[5]

From a structural perspective, sexual relationships between teachers and students cannot be equal, because the roles that define their positions in the system are *inherently* unequal and therefore cannot be made equal. His control over grades and other valued rewards is there for him to use whether he wants to or not, because it is built into the system and the position he occupies in it. Given this, the two people involved may *think* the relationship is based on equality, but they have to pretend that they are somehow above the power of systemically defined relationships to shape the people who participate in them. It may be possible for a healthy relationship to happen in spite of the profound conflict it can generate, but the odds are hugely against it, which is why many organizations and professions discourage or forbid such relationships. It is also why professional norms discourage doctors and therapists from having sexual relationships with patients, or lawyers with clients.

As part of sociological practice, this microlevel view of social structure shows how paths of least resistance shape how we appear and behave. It also points to the difference between what a system looks like and how people choose to participate in it. A role is just a collection of ideas, and there is no way to know exactly how people will behave in relation to them. Therapists and teachers are not supposed to have sex with patients and students, but it has become increasingly apparent that many do anyway. Why?

One reason is that we occupy many different statuses at once. The role of teacher, for example, isn't the only thing that determines whether a professor will initiate a sexual relationship with a student. The fact that the vast majority of sexual harassment and exploitation is perpetrated by men against women suggests something larger going on, especially when we see how prevalent this pattern is in all kinds of systems, from the workplace to the family. Whatever it is that explains why men—and so few women—violate such norms governing the role of teacher won't be found simply by studying the teacher role and how schools are organized as systems. We also have to look at gender as a status and the paths of least resistance that draw men to harass and exploit women in spite of what is expected of them as teachers.

The Personal and the Structural

Most of what we experience in our lives is connected to the structure of one system or another. At first glance, problems that seem to be just a matter of personality or human nature turn out to be at least partly structural, although it's easy to confuse the two. This happens most often with systems we know well, such as families. We experience them in such a personal and immediate way that we may think that's all they amount to, that they aren't systems at all. I have often heard students, for example, state as a matter of obvious fact that their families are unique, that they have no culture or structure, and that they are nothing more than the people who are in them.

Such perceptions make me wonder why they would use the same word— 'family'—to refer to all these groups that supposedly have nothing in common. How is it that family life, for all this uniqueness, looks so remarkably similar from one household to another, such that we can almost always tell a 'family' when we see one? Regardless of each family's idiosyncrasies, they are all families because they are a particular kind of social system that has characteristics that distinguish it from other kinds of systems.

Even if every family were unique, this would not tell us much about the patterns that shape families—and our lives in them—in such recognizable ways. Nor can family 'uniqueness' explain patterns we find among families—the effects of poverty, racism, sexism, and divorce on family life, for example, or what difference it makes whether a family is based on a marriage that's heterosexual, lesbian, gay, or something larger and more communal. Even the most personal emotional problems are increasingly tied to how families work as systems. Many psychotherapists, for example, will not treat adolescent patients without also seeing the rest of the family, because they know that individual troubles don't develop in a vacuum. Our inner emotional lives are never just that—they always happen in relation to a social context.

Abuse in families, for example, is often explained in purely psychological terms. But this ignores research showing that people who abuse children, partners, or the elderly don't have personalities that differ markedly from the rest of the adult population. Extensive research on sexual violence has failed to identify a personality type that distinguishes male perpetrators from 'normal' men. Sexually, men who rape seem to be pretty much like other men and exhibit only a slightly higher propensity toward violent behavior in general. The explanation behind 'intimate violence' won't be found inside the heads and personalities of individuals, because the explanation is both systemic *and* personal.[6]

The simple fact that men commit most serious acts of family violence and sexual exploitation is itself a structural fact of enormous significance. 'Man,' 'husband,' and 'father' are social statuses that are linked to paths of least resistance for the people who occupy them. That so many perpetrators of intimate violence occupy those statuses compels us to ask questions not so much about men as individuals and whether they are good or bad people but, more importantly, about the systems they participate in that load the odds in favor of abusive behavior.

Movies, television, music, video games, and other forms of popular culture, for example, routinely glorify a capacity for control and violence as key traits of 'real men' and denigrate as 'wimps' men who don't measure up. Even presidents worry about being seen as weak and may do foolish things—such as going to war without good reason—to avoid the appearance of being less than strong and decisive. Given this, we shouldn't be surprised to find that men are more likely than women to abuse partners and children.

Abuse is especially likely from men who have more power than their wives in family decision making and from men who are unemployed and cannot measure up to the cultural standard of fulfilling the provider role. In households where abuse occurs, it is more likely to continue if the wife is financially dependent and cannot afford to move out and support the children on her own. Dependence is compounded by the threat of violence itself: it is not uncommon for women to stay in abusive households because they've been threatened with even greater violence if they leave.

Structures of power in family systems create paths of least resistance that make violence far more likely to occur. From this perspective, men's violence against women and girls wouldn't be the epidemic that it currently is in the United States if we lived in a society that supported female independence and gender equality, that valued the health and safety of women and children more than it does, and that didn't promote the capacity for control, domination, and violence as tests of manhood. This doesn't mean that everything is society's fault and that we shouldn't hold individuals accountable when they're abusive. But it does mean that if we want to change pervasive *patterns* of abusive behavior, we have to see how those patterns are connected to paths of least resistance *and* how people choose whether to follow them.

It is also important to consider that a social system can be organized in ways that promote destructive behavior that goes against important cultural values. Consider, for example, such crimes as theft, robbery, and drug deal-ing that people commit to get things they want and cannot otherwise afford to buy. Are people who break the law participating in a society that actually promotes such behavior as a path of least resistance? Robert K. Merton's theory of deviance and opportunity structures responds with a clear "yes."[7]

As Merton points out, capitalist industrial societies place a high value on accumulating possessions. The good life is portrayed as being full of things, and shopping and buying are routinely offered as ways to feel better about ourselves and our lives. No matter which social class you belong to, it's impossible to escape the steady stream of advertising and its underlying message that getting what you do not have is the answer to just about every personal problem.

Although we are all exposed to the cultural value placed on possessions, the distribution of legitimate opportunities to *acquire* them is highly un-equal. Affording many of the goods paraded before mass audiences requires well-paying jobs, which most people do not have. I live near Hartford, Con-necticut, which is one of the poorest cities in the United States while at the same time being the capital city of one of the wealthiest states. For years, on a billboard beside the highway that runs past some of the city's most impov-erished neighborhoods, there was a prominent advertisement for Rolex watches, a brand that typically costs thousands of dollars. I always won-dered how most residents of Hartford were supposed to see this ad in rela-tion to themselves and what they could afford. All kinds of people would drive by that billboard every day and could not help but see its message— this object is what everyone should want to have—but only a select few could afford to buy one. The combination of shared values and an unequal distribution of opportunities makes people more similar in what they're encouraged to *want* than in their ability to *get* what they want in socially acceptable ways.

Being caught in this bind can produce a sense of strain and contradic-tion that people will try to resolve. One way is to work hard in legitimate ways—such as a job—to get what we are all encouraged to want. The op-portunity structure is unequal, however, so this approach works for only a portion of the population, since there aren't enough good jobs to go around. For everyone else, the choices are less appealing. One option is to let go of the cultural value by deciding that possessions aren't so important after all. But this is hard to do since we acquire values at an early age and they are not easy to get rid of, especially when they're being promoted every time we go online, turn on the television, or drive down the interstate.

So, if we cannot stop wanting things and we don't have access to legitimate ways to get them, then what? One answer is what Merton calls 'innovative deviance': if the only way to get a Rolex (or feed our children or wear good clothes) is to break the law, then that is what we'll do. Another response is to rebel by challenging the system and its unequal distribution of opportunities. We might make revolution by demanding a good job for everyone and a redistribution of wealth. Or, we might drop out altogether and move to a cabin in the mountains and try to live off the land, rejecting both the pursuit of possessions and the 'normal' life people live to own things without having to break the law.

The larger the gap is between the distribution of what people are encouraged to want and the distribution of legitimate opportunities for achieving it, the more likely deviance is to occur, whether in the form of innovation, rebellion, or dropping out. This doesn't mean that high crime rates happen because people don't have what they need in some absolute sense. Instead, high crime rates happen because people don't have what others *around* them have and what their culture says they *should* have.

If everyone in a community has the same standard of living, they tend to share values that are consistent with their common condition. But if a community has an impoverished population living next to a wealthy one, theft and other property crimes will be more common because values about wealth are shared but opportunities to acquire it are not. This is exactly what researchers have found. One study, for example, found that rates of burglary and larceny are highest in cities that have the highest levels of income inequality, regardless of the absolute level of poverty.[8] So, communities with high levels of poverty where everyone is pretty much in the same boat will have less crime than communities where people are generally better off but some are much better off than others.

The distribution of values and the distribution of opportunities are characteristics of *systems*, not of individuals who participate in them. In another example, students who cheat are in part responding to how schools are organized as systems. Most school cultures place a high value on grades but do not distribute legitimate ways to achieve them equally. How much encouragement and support students get from their teachers varies considerably by gender, race, ethnicity, and social class. In addition, students differ in how much time and energy for school-related activities they have available (especially when they have to work to support themselves). They also vary in the backgrounds they bring to school, resources available at home, and how much they've been able to develop their abilities and talents. Added to this disparity is the common practice of scaling grades so that a certain percentage of each class must do poorly to round out the low end of the curve. The result is a competitive system with paths of least resistance that motivate students to cheat or 'lower the curve' by sabotaging the work of other students.

This explanation doesn't tell us which students will cheat as they participate in the school system, but it does tell us that we can be sure cheating will occur as a pattern of behavior, because the system loads the odds in that direction. If I flip a fair coin, I can be confident that over the long run, the pattern of results will be roughly equal proportions of tails and heads. Knowing this, however, doesn't tell me what will happen on any given flip. In the same way, knowing how a social system works doesn't tell us how each person is going to participate at any given moment, because sociological practice is not about predicting individual behavior. It is about understanding how social circumstances shape patterns of behavior in one way or another and the consequences that result.

Sociologically, whether a particular student cheats is not the point. That many cheat or only a few, or that the incidence of cheating varies from one kind of school or one social group to another, is. Cheating in school and crime in society are not problems because *this* person cheated or *that* person stole or *this* one wound up living in poverty. What individuals do, of course, matters to us when we are talking about ourselves or people we know. But that is not what alarms us about such problems as poverty, violence, and economic insecurity, which people consistently rank at the top of their concerns. What alarms us is that on some level, we know these problems are rooted in systems we all participate in. As such, they involve all of us, all the time.

Structure as Relation

Statuses are important in the structure of social life because of the relationships that connect them to one another. In a sense, statuses are inherently relational in that they do not exist *except* in relation to other statuses. You cannot describe what a manager, a mother, or a teacher is without referring to some other status, such as employee, daughter, or student. This is true of anything that indicates position and location. 'New York' has no meaning by itself, but it does have meaning in relation to names of other places located by some direction and distance from it. If a community or civilization were to live entirely without awareness of anything beyond itself, naming it is probably the last thing people would think to do.

The relationships that link statuses—or entire systems or parts of systems—to one another are the main part of what we think of as social structure. Seeing how various structural aspects of systems are shaped as people participate in them is a key to sociological practice.

Every system, for example, has a role structure that consists of a mix of statuses and role relationships. The simplest structure consists of the same two statuses in relation to each other, such as two partners in a lesbian marriage. A heterosexual marriage is more complex in that the two statuses are differentiated by gender into wife and husband, and the wife's role in relation to her husband is culturally defined as different from his role in relation to her. In either case, a marriage system can change radically by adding just one more status—that of child—to the mix, as new parents know all too well.

Adding a child to a heterosexual marriage adds not only that status but also the statuses of mother and father. As a result, the role structure goes from two statuses to five, and the number of role relationships goes from one to eight even though only three people participate in the system (see Figures 2 and 3). Life suddenly becomes far more complicated and causes familiar patterns of stress and confusion.

A girl's father, for example, is also her mother's husband, and a wife's husband is also her child's father. In such a system, whom people communicate with, whom they pay attention to, whose needs they meet in a given moment, and how they feel about one another all emerge from a complex interplay of several paths of least resistance operating at once. Men's jealousy over the attention their wives (who are also mothers, but not theirs) pay to newborn children is the best known of these structural phenomena that happen so often because family structures load the odds in that direction. If, instead, every household had numerous adults available for child care, family dynamics would be very different than they are in typical two-adult nuclear families based on heterosexual marriage.

Figure 2. Role structure of a heterosexual marriage.

Figure 3. Role structure of a heterosexual marriage with one child.

Family role structures can be complicated further by exchanging a step-parent for a birth parent. This happens in every family organized around a remarriage for one or both spouses. With children related by birth to only one spouse and to a parent who no longer lives in the household, the potential for conflict and bad feelings is built in to the system. Until stepparents develop their own place in the new family, they can feel left out and be denied loyalty, affection, and respect from stepchildren. Competition can also erupt over the attention and loyalty of the birth parent, who feels torn between the children and the new partner. Coalitions against the stepparent—children and either birth parent ganging up against the newcomer—are always a danger, especially when children still hope to bring their birth parents back together.

None of this structural information tells us just what will happen in each individual family. It does, however, tell us a lot about built-in paths of least resistance and where they are likely to lead family dynamics when people follow them. When stepparents feel rejected and unwelcome by stepchildren, for example, they are bound to take it personally. But they might take comfort from knowing that the system's structure sets things up to go this way until a new structure emerges from the interactions of daily life, which are in turn shaped by how each member of the family chooses to participate.

We can do this kind of analysis on every social system from the smallest and simplest to the largest and most complex, from the flow of information in business and government to problems of command and control in the military or a terrorist organization, from the success or failure of social movements to the role structure of urban gangs, from the structure of international conflict and the global economy to the changing relations between doctors and patients in managed-care health systems. The basic questions about how structure shapes social life remain the same.

We can ask, for example, about the roles of industrial and nonindustrial societies in the world economy and how these lead to a widening gap between rich and poor nations and increased levels of inequality within them as well, all of which can encourage resistance movements, including those that resort to terrorism and other violent means. We can also ask how global dynamics affect the small scale of family life as corporations maximize profit and returns paid to investors by closing factories and moving jobs from one place to another or by hiring people on a part-time basis only, with lower pay and no benefits. Sociological practice always takes us toward the vital and difficult truth that everything is related in one way or another to everything else. This truth is what makes the practice so challenging, but it is also what gives it such great promise.

Structure as Distribution: Who Gets What

We saw earlier that a heterosexual marriage has a more complex structure than does a lesbian or gay marriage because of gender distinctions between wives and husbands. The differences do not stop there, however, because the concept of structure also includes various kinds of distributions in systems.

In most societies, for example, husbands tend to have more power, reflecting the privileged position of men in general in patriarchal societies. Like all social systems, families have resources and rewards that are distributed among the people who participate in them. The most important of these are power, income, wealth, and prestige, but they could include a variety of other benefits as well, such as parental attention or access to material culture, such as cars. Whatever the resources and rewards are in a particular system, the basic structural questions remain: how unequal is the distribution, how is that accomplished, how is the pattern of inequality justified and maintained, and how does all this affect people and the system as a whole by producing various kinds of consequences?

In most patriarchal societies, male privilege is supported by a culture in which boys are seen as more important and valuable than girls. In many societies, the birth of a boy is celebrated, while the birth of a girl is seen as a disappointment if not a catastrophe. Even in the United States, when people are asked which gender they would rather have if they could have only one child, boys are still 43 percent more likely to be preferred than girls.[9]

Male privilege is most apparent in the unequal distribution of resources within the family. In China, for example, girl babies may be left to die after birth or survive into childhood only to be sold off into marriage or prostitution, a sex trade that is now global, including Europe and the United States. In nineteenth-century Ireland, the survival rate for girls was considerably below that of boys primarily because of how food and other resources were distributed in families.[10]

Both within and among societies today, patterns of social inequality are major features of how social systems work, whether based on class, gender, race, disability status, ethnicity, age, or sexual orientation. At the heart of these patterns is the distribution of power. Power is one of the most important concepts in sociological practice but also one of the most difficult to work with, because there are several ways to define it. The standard definition comes from the nineteenth-century German sociologist Max Weber, who is perhaps best known for his prophetic work on bureaucracy. According to Weber, bureaucracy is a way of organizing and applying a particular kind of power, and his work correctly predicted that it would become the dominant form of social organization in virtually every aspect of social life from school to religion to government.

Weber defines power as the ability to control events, resources, and people in spite of opposition—in other words, as a means of control, coercion, and domination. Although this form of power is certainly the one most valued in today's societies, it is not the only possibility. There is, for example, the power to cooperate and share or to nurture and facilitate processes that we do not control. Midwives play a powerful role in the birth process, for example, but they do not control it or dominate the people involved in it. There is also the powerful experience of coming together with other people in religious and community rituals that affirm a sense of belonging and meaning in life. Related to this is spiritual power that often comes from deeply moving life experiences and forms of spiritual practice that people experience as extraordinarily powerful, but not in a coercive or controlling way.

In a patriarchal world, however, the human capacity to control has been elevated to such a lofty position that 'power' and 'powerful' invariably look more like Weber's meaning than its alternatives. Given the fact that the world is largely organized around this form of power, and given the huge social consequences this produces—especially in the form of privilege and oppression—Weber's definition is the one used most often in sociology.

Systems and Systems: Family and Economy

Nothing in social life can be understood without seeing its connections to other aspects of social life, a principle that applies within systems and among them. If we compare family life two centuries ago with family life today, for example, we find dramatic differences caused in part by equally dramatic changes in the organization of economic life.

Before the rise of industrial capitalism in the eighteenth and nineteenth centuries, most goods in the United States were produced by families primarily for their own use. People grew and raised much of what they ate, made everything from clothes to candles, and bartered for whatever else they needed. The same patterns were found in most of what we think of today as 'services.' What people couldn't do for themselves, they did cooperatively with neighbors—from raising barns to bringing in crops—or traded, service for service. Money played a small part, typically used to settle accounts at the end of the year when someone had done more for someone else than had been done for them.

The patriarchal family power structure was based primarily on male ownership of land, but what actually went on in families centered on women, because they were responsible for most productive work, including raising children. Men monopolized certain areas of production, such as the cultivation of fields, but most of the goods and services that family members used and consumed—clothing, food, candles, soap, and the like—were produced by women.

Women, then, occupied a contradictory position—subordinate in the power structure but indispensable in the role structure. To some degree, the interdependence between men and women may have dampened the effects of patriarchal domination, for most men needed women too much to take full advantage of their authority as head of the family.

These family role structures also held an important place for children. Since most people lived on farms, children began working at an early age. When public schooling was introduced on a wide scale in the mid- and late-nineteenth century, the vacation calendar was organized around the family's need for child labor during the growing and harvest seasons, which is why schooling stopped for the summer. Since children routinely worked alongside parents and other adults, there was plenty of chance for interaction across generations, especially with fathers and mothers. While raising children was still primarily a mother's responsibility, with families living and working in the same place, fathers also had reason to take an active interest in their children's development.[11]

The structures of work and family life changed with the rise of industrial capitalism, and the effects are still with us today. As people left farms to work in urban factories, living and working in the same place became increasingly a thing of the past. This created a dilemma for parents that had never existed before in human experience: they could not do economically productive work and take care of their children at the same time. Many lower- and working-class families could not survive without the earnings of both spouses, so children had to fend for themselves in many ways. But in the expanding middle of the class system, the dilemma was resolved by keeping wives at home while husbands went to work for wages.

As is so often the case, the patterns found in the middle and upper classes became general cultural ideals, and working-class husbands and fathers increasingly measured their success by the ability to support their families on their own and 'keep' their wives and children at home. This is one reason why male workers demanded and eventually won a family wage that allowed a man to support an entire family with his earnings alone. This was more than a concession to labor, for it also helped men maintain their dominant position in the family.[12]

The characteristics of the industrial capitalist system, then, radically split the typical family role structure. The productive work that women had done—from baking bread to making soap to weaving cloth—was rapidly taken over by industries that could do it faster and cheaper. This meant that for the first time, child care became a full-time job for middle-class women, along with certain kinds of domestic work, such as cleaning. Increasingly, children spent most of their time with mothers, and husbands and wives no longer worked side by side.

Shifting production from home to factory also affected children's roles within the family and elsewhere. Putting children to work in factories provided extra family income, but it also put children in competition with adults. This, along with concern for how easily children were exploited with long hours of work and poor wages under terrible conditions, resulted in legal bans on child labor, with compulsory schooling taking its place. As children lost their place in the adult work world, 'adolescence' emerged as a developmental stage between childhood and adulthood, along with dramatic changes in cultural views of young people. As children lost their economic value in families, for example, their emotional value to parents increased.[13]

But children's dependent emotional attachment to parents was not—and still is not—enough to replace an active productive role in family life. Until industrial capitalism transformed the world, children in every society were productive members of their families. When children lost this position, they needed something to replace it to feel a sense of worth and belonging.

The answer was an expanding peer culture isolated from the surrounding adult culture and often at odds with it. Adolescence has become a growing source of deviant and often violent behavior as adolescents reject mainstream cultural values. Adolescent males, for example, account for more criminal behavior than any other age group. As Margaret Mead argues in her classic study of adolescence in Samoa, such patterns may reflect the broad historical shifts in the structure of family and economic life and how these shifts have deprived young people of a secure and meaningful place in their families and in society.[14]

In several ways, then, the industrial capitalist system has undermined the positions of women and children. It has also affected men, although in different ways and degrees.[15] The shift of production out of the home and away from agriculture virtually destroyed the family as an economically productive system, at least as far as society and its rewards were concerned. What goes on in families is still critical to what goes on in the economy, since without families there would be no place for workers to be cared for and nurtured. There would also be no place for future workers to be raised into adulthood. But this contribution is rarely recognized as a form of productive work with economic value.

As a result of the capitalist Industrial Revolution, owning land and dominating the family no longer amounted to much as a basis for men's patriarchal authority. In other words, men were now the 'heads' of something that had lost most of its importance as a source of prestige and power. The world was still patriarchal and organized in male-dominated, male-identified, and male-centered ways, but the position of individual men *within* that world shifted dramatically. Most men no longer had any authority over production—as men once had as farmers or independent artisans—but now worked for wages under conditions controlled by employers. This shift meant that men had to find other ways to secure and exercise male privilege.

One answer was for men to control the wages they earned and what families purchased with them. Women, for example, were not allowed to own property, sign contracts, or spend money they earned. Men, however, enjoyed an independence they had not known before. A capitalist economy based on wages allowed people to survive as individuals by earning money outside the family. This broke the powerful economic interdependency that had previously bound women, men, and children together in a productive family system.

Because male privilege allowed men to avoid taking care of children, men could—and did—take advantage of this possibility for independence in ways that women could not. Many people today believe this arrangement in which men work outside as family providers and women stay home and do not 'work' is the natural way of organizing family life that has always been around in one form or another in every society. In fact, however, this social invention was extraordinarily recent and did not dominate for very long, as the massive entry of wives, mothers, and other women into the paid labor force during the second half of the twentieth century shows.

In many ways, women are completing a transformation of family role structures that men began more than a century ago. In this sense, working women do not represent a radical departure from traditional family life. Women have always worked in economically productive ways, and men were, in fact, the first to introduce the idea of parents working apart from their children. The pattern of wives and mothers working outside the home is part of a long-term adaptation by families to an industrial capitalist world that, like every society before it, requires most adults to work for families to survive.

Men leaving home for work during the capitalist Industrial Revolution created strains in family life, and women's exit from a strictly domestic role is having similar effects, especially on child care. This situation is not simply a result of the women's movement or because women now choose to work outside the home more than they did before. It results from an ongoing tension between economic and family structures, a tension that was first resolved—for a while and in certain social classes—by keeping wives and mothers at home and financially dependent on their husbands. As wives and mothers move into paid work outside the home, the old ways of resolving that tension will not work, which is why a child-care crisis exists in the United States (except for families wealthy enough to hire women to take care of their children for them).

The ability of large numbers of adults to earn a living without being tied to a family system of production was unheard of before the capitalist Industrial Revolution. When such independence became possible, it changed the shape of family life and the relationships of women, men, and children to one another. Today, the percentage of people who live alone and the percentages of men and women in their late twenties who have never married are increasing steadily, following rapid increases during the preceding decades. Nonfamily households are being created at a rate twice that of family households.[16] At the same time, employers are beginning to feel pressure to do something to relieve the strain felt by family members who must work. How this situation plays out will depend in large part on a willingness to ask difficult questions about what families are, why they matter, and what an economic system is supposed to provide for the people who participate in it.

The Structure-Culture Connection

The concepts of culture and social structure are tools, devices for thinking about social life in ways that help reveal how things work. They are useful because they focus attention on different aspects of reality so that we can then reassemble them in our minds into a coherent whole. Because culture and structure have their own names and are typically discussed separately, they are often thought to be separate in reality as well—culture over here, structure over there.

However, as I pointed out at the end of Chapter 1, we never find one without the other, because everything in social life, from people to systems, exists only in relation to something else. Understanding what culture and structure *are*, then, is just the beginning, because we also must see how they shape social life in relation to each other and the people who participate in systems.

We can think of racial prejudice, for example, as a cultural attitude that combines stereotyped beliefs about different races and values that rank some as superior. People who don't qualify as white are viewed as inferior to those who do, and lighter skin is preferred over darker.

Prejudice would not be such a problem if it were not connected to structural aspects of societies, especially role structures—who gets to do what—and the distribution of power, prestige, and other resources and rewards. Prejudice would cause little more than hurt feelings if it were not for systematic patterns of inequality in economic and legal systems, in political power, in how children are treated in school and pedestrians on the street, in access to health care and all kinds of social services that affect the quality of life. In this sense, racism is not just a way of thinking or feeling. Racism is an integral part of the structure of entire social systems that privilege and empower some groups at the expense of others.

We can look at cultural prejudice as both a consequence and a cause of structural inequality. Negative prejudice about black people in the United States, for example, makes it a path of least resistance for white people to treat them badly or allow such treatment to go on unchallenged. But the effect also works in the other direction: if white people treat black people badly as part of asserting white privilege, then white people can use negative views of black people to rationalize such behavior and make the privilege seem appropriate or not even privilege at all. This makes ending racism more than just a matter of changing habitual ways of thinking or feeling about race. It also involves a complex set of structural arrangements that shape the system of white privilege, and getting white people to give up *this* is a much larger and more difficult task.

If black people were not concentrated in the lower and working classes, for example, they would give middle-class white people much more competition over jobs and would not be available to capitalist businesses as a source of cheap labor. It is unlikely that white people or capitalist enterprise would welcome that kind of racial progress. This makes it easier to focus on cultural prejudice as the sole problem rather than on the structures of white privilege and capitalist economics that prejudice supports. No matter how much we succeed at changing racism's cultural aspects, we still must find a way to deal with its structure.[17]

Cultural and structural aspects of racism are connected not only in how they work but also in their dynamics of change. Stereotyped beliefs about race, for example, are organized around real or imagined differences that are distorted and exaggerated to benefit one race at the expense of others. The beliefs are generalized to every member of the target group and are usually seen as inherent—people are the way they are simply because they belong to that racial group. Since the beliefs rarely describe actual people with any accuracy, the best way to undermine those beliefs is to give people a chance to experience people of different races and see what they are really like. But this cannot happen as long as people live and work in segregated communities. In the United States, for example, neighborhoods and schools are so segregated by race that a large portion of students would have to move for the percentage of each racial group in schools to match its percentage in the population as a whole.[18]

Racial isolation makes it easy to perpetuate stereotypes, because people never have to test them against reality. If we change the structure of race relations, however, by creating opportunities for people to work and study together, we make it easier for stereotypes to fall apart in the face of hard evidence about what people are really like.[19] In this way, integration lessens racial stereotyping and increases cross-race friendship, especially when people work together on teams and depend on one another to accomplish goals they have in common. This is one reason why the military and athletic teams have generally done a better job of dealing with racism than other systems.

The interplay between culture and structure is fundamental to social life, as when a shift in cultural values prompts a shift in the structural distribution of power. At several points in the history of education in the United States, for example, the value placed on student autonomy and personal growth increased so much that the power structure in many schools shifted to give students greater control over what they studied and how.

Structural shifts can also stimulate cultural change. As recently as the 1960s, divorce was still considered to be so shameful that it could ruin a political career. As the number of divorced people grew, however, they became more visible, and divorce became more socially acceptable and therefore less of a liability.

Similar cultural shifts are occurring around sexual orientation as gays, lesbians, and bisexuals come out and increase their visibility as members of families, communities, workplaces, schools, and places of worship. Acceptance of same-sex marriage increased dramatically between 2003 and 2013, with one of the main causes being the increase in the number of heterosexuals who know someone who is lesbian, gay, or bisexual.[20]

Such patterns show how different aspects of social systems can both reinforce and contradict one another, producing strain that changes paths of least resistance. Patterns of privilege and oppression continue in part because they conform to powerful cultural ideas about the superiority of men, whites, heterosexuals, and other dominant groups. Those same patterns, however, also violate important cultural values about equal opportunity, fairness, tolerance, freedom, and respect for differences.

This kind of contradiction has produced for the United States what Gunnar Myrdal calls "an American dilemma"[21] that forces people to confront the fact that a way of life that includes racism violates some of the nation's most cherished values. Martin Luther King Jr. and others in the civil rights movement used this contradiction as a powerful source of leverage during the 1950s and 1960s. Rather than calling on white people to change cultural values, they instead challenged white people to honor and live up to existing values. This approach forced many white people to make a choice between such values as fairness and equal opportunity on the one hand and the ongoing reality of racism and white privilege on the other. As Myrdal predicted, the resulting tension continues to produce pressure for change.

The role of contradiction in social life was first seriously explored by Karl Marx, who developed it into a major part of his analysis of how capitalism works as a system.[22] Capitalism is organized around a core set of relationships between (1) machinery, tools, factories, and other means of production, (2) those who own or control the means of production (capitalists, corporate managers, and investors), and (3) the workers who do not own or control the means of production but use them to produce wealth in return for wages. Capitalists profit from this arrangement by keeping for themselves a portion of the value that workers produce. Workers get what they need by holding onto as much of that value as they can. So, if workers produce $5 million worth of goods above the cost of materials and other expenses, they get to keep only a portion of that value for themselves, with the rest going to capitalists and investors.

Marx sees this arrangement as inherently contradictory. In the simplest sense, the interests of workers and capitalists conflict—each succeeds only at the expense of the other in what is essentially an exploitative relationship. In a related sense, capitalists are encouraged to keep as much for themselves as they can to increase their wealth. But if capitalists keep too much, workers won't have enough money to buy what they produce, which defeats the very purpose of the economic system and precipitates a crisis.

In a third sense, the capitalist system is contradictory in its drive for economic efficiency—producing the most wealth for the lowest cost. In the typical capitalist society, efficiency is measured as the cost of producing each product (each car, each bushel of wheat) in terms of the number of hours of labor it requires. If efficiency improves, this means that workers are producing more each hour *but without being paid proportionately more* as a result. Producing twice as much per hour, in other words, does not result in being paid twice as much.

The more efficient and productive workers are, the worse off they are in that their *share* of the total wealth they produce goes down. This explains in part what has happened in the United States since the 1980s—productivity and corporate profits have increased while workers' incomes have stayed the same or actually declined as the overall level of social inequality has gone up. Between 1994 and 1995, for example, the median household income increased faster than the rate of inflation for the first time in six years but was still below the average for 1989. When only employment earnings are counted, median earnings actually fell.[23] Since 1999, adjusting for inflation, average household income has fallen each year.[24]

From Marx's perspective, the only remedy for such contradictions is to change the structure of capitalism itself—the relations between workers, owners, and the means of production—and the relationship between capitalism and other institutions, especially the state. But such change threatens the basis of privilege enjoyed by the capitalist class. Since the capitalist class has a great deal of power and political influence, the idea of changing the structure of capitalism runs into fierce opposition any time it is suggested, as happened to the Occupy Wall Street movement in 2011 and 2012. As a result, the contradictions are never resolved and the system is kept stable by other means, especially through the power of the state. Early in the twentieth century, for example, the labor-union movement ran into stiff and often violent opposition from employers. Federal and state governments often stepped in with troops and police to protect the private property rights of owners of factories, trains, and other capital.

Intervention of this kind continues today, although in ways less likely to involve the overt use of force (except in emerging capitalist industrial societies, such as South Korea). After the 2008 crisis in the financial industry, for example, the federal government provided tens of billions of dollars to protect large banks from failing, and declined to prosecute bank officials who engaged in illegal practices that caused the crisis and ensuing financial loss for tens of millions of people.[25]

The state also uses its resources to soften capitalism's negative consequences for workers with such programs as unemployment compensation, Social Security, welfare and medical benefits, low-interest mortgages, college loans, occupational safety regulations, and laws that forbid unfair labor practices and regulate the flow of immigrants who might compete for jobs. All these benefits are necessary because of consequences produced by capitalism. If workers were able to keep more of the value of what they produce and full employment were a serious national goal, there would be less need for welfare and unemployment compensation. And if the profit motive and competition that underlie capitalism did not encourage employers to relentlessly cut costs, there would be less need for federal regulations to require businesses to spend money to ensure a safe environment for workers.

This kind of counterbalancing of one part of a system (such as the economy) by another (such as the state) can stabilize and perpetuate systems at all levels of social life. When a marriage is in trouble, for example, it's not unusual for couples to have a child in the belief that this will bring them closer together. In other words, they change the family's structure to keep it going. In more subtle ways, spouses may change the family role structure to compensate for a dysfunctional relationship. Children, for example, may be drawn into a situation in which a parent expects them to meet the parent's needs in inappropriate ways, in extreme cases sexually as well as emotionally. This kind of triangulation can continue for years as part of a family system in spite of the damage it does to children. In each case—whether capitalist economics or the family—structural strain in one part of the system is connected to changes in another.

Systems within Systems

Much of the focus on social structure centers on statuses as 'parts' that make up systems. This is especially true of role relationships. But as the relationship between capitalism and the state shows, we can also look at what goes on *between* systems, where systems themselves are parts of still larger systems.

To understand something like stress in families, for example, it makes sense to begin with the family itself. Families in industrial capitalist societies experience all kinds of stress and strain—worry about making ends meet, buying a home, keeping up with the mortgage, sending children to college, getting good health care, taking care of children when both parents have to work, coping with emotional problems, the threat of divorce, and patterns of violence and abuse. Looking at the family as a system, we can ask how it works and how family members participate in ways that ease such problems or make them worse.

The nuclear family structure, for example, places a heavy burden on just two adults, a burden that would not be nearly as hard to carry if it were spread out among many adults, as in extended families. On an individual level, men's willingness to shoulder their share of responsibility for household work can make a huge difference in family life, beginning with the level of stress and strain on working wives and mothers and their relation to husbands and fathers. That choice, of course, is influenced by a larger system in which male privilege exempts men from having to feel responsible for such tasks, however willing they may be to 'help out' when asked.

Since everything is always connected to other things, we cannot understand what goes on in a family by looking *just* at the family. We also have to see how the family and its members exist in relation to other and often larger systems. The family survives in relation to an economy in which goods and services are produced and distributed. When the economy is organized to value profit above the welfare of people who participate in it, conflicting interests are built into the relation between economy and family.

Investors, for example, do not buy stock in companies as a way to provide jobs for people who, in turn, can then support families and raise children. Investors invest as a way to take surplus money and turn it into more money, and the most efficient way to do that under capitalism often results in a *loss* of jobs and dislocation and strain in families and communities. Family life is affected by forces far beyond the family itself when corporations lay off workers and send jobs overseas to make themselves more competitive and profitable in relation to other corporations, or when wages don't keep up with inflation and both spouses are forced to work outside the home. The stress that so many families experience today isn't just about the family but also about structured relations that connect the family to other systems.

Such patterns are found in every social system. Towns and cities, for example, are related to one another and to larger systems, such as counties, states, provinces, and societies, and those relationships profoundly affect what goes on within them. We cannot understand the crisis of U.S. inner cities without looking at the relationship between cities and suburbs. In many large cities, school systems are desperate for money, and student populations are overwhelmingly of color and lower and working class. This combination all but ensures continued inequality in education and training.

Part of the problem is that each community is responsible for funding its own schools. As middle-class people migrate to the suburbs, urban populations become increasingly impoverished and unable to provide for basic services, including education. One structural solution is to redraw school-district lines in ways that spread the load of educating children more broadly. If school districts were based on counties or regions, for example, then a city and all its suburbs would be considered one large school district, and funding would be spread evenly throughout.

Where the lines that define school districts are drawn is a matter of structural boundaries that define school districts in relation to political systems. It changes the definition of who is responsible for what, of what 'we' means when we say things like, "We're in this together," and who is included in the responsibility to educate 'our' children. And when political boundaries determine how financial responsibility is distributed, they also touch on the structural distribution of wealth, which is a major reason why suburban communities resist enlarging the boundaries of school districts.

Given the relation of systems to other systems, we need to expand the basic principle of sociological practice we began with in Chapter 1. Not only do individuals always participate in something larger than themselves, but those 'somethings'—those systems—also exist in relation to something larger than *them*selves. To do this kind of work, it is important to think across the different levels on which social life happens, to see how groups are connected to organizations and communities, how organizations and communities are connected to societies, how societies are connected to one another, and how individuals participate in it all.

4

Population and Human Ecology

People, Space, and Place

Most sociologists see social life as a matter of culture, social structure, and the interaction through which people participate in systems. But this view leaves out the fact that social life always happens some *place* and involves some number of people.

We could describe an office where people work, for example, as a system having beliefs, values, norms, a role structure, distributions of power and income, and so on. And we could look at how people use language and behavior to interact and make the office system happen from one day to the next. Suppose, however, the company downsizes by cutting the number of workers by a third. What changes then, and how do we make sense of it?

The system's structure is the same—the same roles to be performed and the same unequal distribution of power and rewards. The culture is also unchanged—same rules and goals as before. What has changed is the number of people who participate in the system, and, as anyone who survives a layoff knows, the effects of this change can be profound, as fewer people must do the work once done by many more, and usually with no increase in compensation. They may have a mix of feelings—lucky to have a job at all or guilty in relation to those who no longer do, followed by anxiety and depression over what might happen next, knowing that no job is secure. They may also be suspicious of management that seems to care more about stockholders and the bottom line than about people who have been with the company for many years. Such feelings, in turn, can affect the entire system, as cynicism, resentment, and fear emerge as prevailing attitudes in the worker subculture.

Numbers count, from the smallest level of social life to the largest. Every teacher and student knows how much it matters whether a class has five students or five hundred, how difficult discussion is in the latter, and how much pressure there is to participate in the former. And we are having to learn rapidly about the problems linked to an expanding global population, especially in parts of the world least equipped to clothe and feed the people who live there. Whether the numbers are figured in tens or in billions, we need tools to see how they affect social life and its consequences.

We also need ways to pay attention to the fact that systems and people exist not in the abstract but in a material world of space and objects. If five students in a seminar are seated around a small table, for example, the conversation will be much more productive than if they're scattered about an auditorium where they have to shout to be heard. If they are seated in a circle of chairs with no desks or tables to separate them, the conversation is likely to be more personal, which is why I often use this arrangement to talk about sensitive topics, such as privilege and oppression, so that participants will be aware of how they feel as well as what they think. On a larger level, spatial arrangements matter just as profoundly. White privilege, for example, depends on the physical segregation of different racial groups, an arrangement that reinforces the structure of privilege and helps maintain racial stereotypes by minimizing contact across races. In this way, millions of people are literally kept in their place.

Part of the human relation to space and place is a matter of physical arrangements, from residential segregation to the placement of furniture in a room. But that relation also has to do with how people use the materials found in physical environments, especially natural resources. A college classroom, for example, reflects a complex relation between social systems and the physical world, from using materials to make furniture and audio-visual equipment to drilling for oil to burn in furnaces that heat classrooms, to using nuclear power to generate electricity to run computers and lighting. The classroom also reflects a world in which the system of production is so efficient that a small number of people grow enough food for everyone and millions of people can spend their days reading books and learning to think in new ways instead of working in agriculture.

Social reality, in short, always includes a biological and material reality. Numbers count. Space, place, and geography matter. People are born in numbers large and small and migrate from place to place. The stuff of the Earth is transformed into the endless shapes and forms that humans are capable of giving it. This is the material reality of population and human ecology, and paying attention to it can inform and deepen almost every sort of sociological practice.

Human Ecology

Social life revolves around people, social systems, and the relationships among them. But those are not the only relations that matter, for people and social systems exist in relation to physical environments. Human ecology is the study of those relationships, and it figures in social life at every level.[1]

In the colonial period of U.S. history, for example, the typical home was arranged around a single fireplace, which was the only source of heat. This naturally drew family members to one room during the winter months, which encouraged conversation, storytelling, and other ways of being together. With the invention of central heating, every room in the house was equally warm, which removed a major reason for people to spend time together on a regular basis.

In similar ways, physical arrangements shape every social interaction. Office cubicles that lack doors and walls reaching to the ceiling, for example, make privacy impossible and signal a corresponding lack of autonomy, status, and power in an organization. In families, men are more likely than women to have rooms of their own (if there's a study or a workshop, it's more likely to be his than hers). As the late British novelist Virginia Woolf argues in her classic book *A Room of One's Own*, without a protected space in which to work, women writers could not develop their art, which is one reason why, historically, so few women emerged as prominent writers.[2]

Every social situation has an ecological angle. Typical classrooms, for example, are arranged to reinforce the teacher's authority by facing students' chairs toward the front so that it's harder for students to interact with one another than with the teacher. In courtrooms and churches, judges and clergy are typically elevated above everyone else in a physical arrangement that underscores and reinforces differences in power and status. Both houses of the U.S. Congress are arranged much like large college lecture halls, with leaders at the front on elevated platforms, an arrangement that both bows to the idea of hierarchy and makes spirited debate all but impossible. In the British House of Commons, by contrast, opposing parties are seated across from one another in a relatively small and confined space, which makes face-to-face debate almost unavoidable.[3]

Ecology also figures in the arrangement of larger settings, such as neighborhoods and communities. In comparison with cities in Europe and Latin America, for example, the United States has relatively few public spaces, such as parks, squares, and sidewalk cafes, where people can greet and socialize with one another outside their homes. Without such spaces, it becomes harder to sustain a sense of community, a sense of common ground on which to meet and feel the presence of other members of the community.

Residential segregation by race, class, and ethnicity is another ecological arrangement that profoundly affects social life, especially in perpetuating privilege and oppression.[4] Physical separation makes it easier to maintain stereotypes; leads to an unequal distribution of community services, such as schools and police protection; and gives a physical dimension to the unequal distribution of opportunities by separating working- and lower-class people from better jobs, which are often located away from the central city. Segregation also shapes patterns of behavior, such as criminal victimization. Most violent crime in the United States, for example, is intraracial, because opportunities for physical contact are far more common within races than between them. Similar dynamics help explain why such a large percentage of violence happens within families and other intimate relationships rather than between strangers.

Every social system, then, includes a sense of place and space (including cyberspace), and this shapes how we perceive and behave toward one another. The Internet, for example, allows people to interact from a position of anonymity, presenting themselves—their gender, race, age, and name, for example—however they want. This, in turn, makes it easier for people to say things they would not say to someone face-to-face, and online harassment and bullying have become increasingly common as a result.

Social systems also exist in relation to the Earth and the species that inhabit it. To look at those relationships, ecologists use the concept of an 'ecosystem,' which is defined by a given space and its inhabitants. That space can be defined in just about any way we want. We could think of a drop of pond water as an ecosystem, for example, or a chunk of soil in a field, the city of Toronto, or the entire universe. Where we draw the line depends primarily on what we want to know about. Sociologically, what is most important to see is how human populations live in relation to one another and their physical surroundings, the consequences this produces, and for whom or what.

Ecologically, we are just like any other life-form. We reproduce, we live by using and consuming what is around us, and we die. Like many species, we move about and build things. Just as caribou migrate with the seasons, people migrate to escape wars or natural disasters or to find employment or get married. Birds build nests, and people build houses. We stand out in our ability to transform the Earth and our place in it in ways that are much more profound and drastic than other species. In addition to being the only species that cultivates its own food, for example, we may be one of the few that systematically tries to kill off all its competitors.

Humans also use technology to get around the natural conditions that otherwise limit population growth. For every other species, when there is too little food to go around, populations get smaller through higher death rates and lower birth rates. But human dominance of the Earth has promoted cultural values and beliefs that make this unacceptable, so humans have continued to reproduce and exploit natural resources as if there were no natural limit to what we might do or how many of us there might be. Global warming promises to impose just such a limit, the consequences of which are already beginning to be felt, especially in colder regions of the Earth.[5] Meanwhile, other species cannot respond and adapt to the changes caused by our use of complex technology and are left to survive as best they can, which, to judge by the accelerating rate at which they are becoming extinct, is none too good.

In such ways, social systems profoundly affect ecosystems. But this also works in the other direction, as ecosystems shape the culture and structure of systems. Anthropologist Marvin Harris, for example, is a cultural materialist who argues that many aspects of human cultures come about in response to material conditions in the natural environment. They are practical adaptations to the natural world even when they may not seem so. Harris tries to identify, for example, an ecological basis for the Hindu religious prohibition against the eating of beef,[6] a cultural practice that seems to many Westerners to be irrational in a country, such as India, whose people need all the food they can get.

But Harris says that just the opposite is true. Historically, rice has been the primary food grown in India, and the cow played an important role in producing it. Rice grows in fields that are often under water, and the cow (unlike the horse) has a cloven hoof that doesn't get stuck by suction in the mud of the fields. Cows also produce dung that can serve many purposes, from fuel to fertilizer to bricks for building.

The cow, then, has been an extraordinarily useful animal in the history of India's agricultural economy. But the ecological angle to the cow's sacred status is more complicated, involving also India's climate, which includes periodic droughts and equally devastating famines. During these times, farm families who would eat their cattle as a last resort would solve their food problem in the short run, but only by destroying what they would need to cultivate crops when the rains returned. What could be powerful enough to keep families from giving in to the temptation to eat their cows during such desperate times? Harris answers that India's culture evolved to protect the cow—and, therefore, the long-term welfare of India's people—by giving the cow a sacred status that no religious person would dare violate. From an ecological perspective, what Westerners might view as an irrational waste of animal protein may have been an adaptation to a difficult environment.

We could apply similar reasoning to the heavy consumption of beef in the United States. Cultivating millions of acres to grow corn to feed beef cattle is a relatively inefficient use of land, because only a portion of the nutrition in the corn that cattle eat actually winds up as food for people. If that same land were used to cultivate crops that humans consumed directly (such as grains and beans), the result would be far more nutrition than beef provides. So far, the United States has been able to afford such levels of inefficiency because a favorable climate supports huge agricultural surpluses. India's experience, however, suggests that with climate change, the day will come when that is no longer true.

To a cultural materialist like Harris, every social system is shaped as it adapts to physical conditions in its environment. But as we've seen, this dynamic works both ways. Most species occupy very specialized places in the food chain. They eat only a few kinds of foods and alter the environment (such as by building nests) in relatively small ways. By comparison, human societies have the potential to affect the environment in ways both huge and complex. People eat all kinds of food and change the shape and composition of earth, air, and water in so many ways that it's impossible to keep track of them, much less understand the consequences they produce. Technology enables us to not only irrigate fields, build cities, and pollute the air, water, and soil but also alter genetic structures.

Some cultures regard these abilities as part of a human destiny to rule the Earth. The complexity of ecosystems, however, suggests that people have far less control than they might think. Humans have a much greater ability than other species to affect the environment, but we usually do not discover the consequences of what we've done until long after the fact. This lag means that we also have a much greater ability to do harm and damage and are the only ones in a position to prevent it. Only we can save us (and everyone else) from ourselves.

Notice for a moment the language that is often used to talk about how societies affect the environment. Like all symbols, such words as 'harm' and 'damage' reflect a particular cultural view of reality—in this case, the reality of 'nature' and our relation to it. To say that the environment is being destroyed, for example, means that certain states of nature that are rated highly in cultural value systems are at risk. Those values, however, are inherent not in nature but in human cultures. Ecosystems do not value one condition over another, in that a lake full of fish is no less natural or desirable from the environment's point of view than is a lake full of algae.

For that matter, nature also does not value humanity over any other species of life. Life is life. If we look at the vast majority of the Earth's 4.6 billion years of existence, ecosystems were dominated by what human cultures classify as lower life-forms. As far as we know, over the first 2.6 billion years of the Earth's history there was no life at all, and for the next billion years nothing more than simple bacteria and algae. Single-celled protozoa appeared only 800 million years ago (after more than 80 percent of the Earth's history had already gone by), and multicelled blue-green algae colonies developed only 600 million years ago. What we think of as plants are only about 500 million years old, and mammals only 200 million years old. In short, the Earth took the vast majority of its existence to go from a state of no life at all to what we would call a swamp. Only in its most recent past—a blink of an eye in relative terms—has the Earth started to look like what most of us think of as 'nature.'

If we take the long view, ecosystems cannot be damaged or destroyed. They can change their characteristics, including the mix of different forms of life they can support (which may or may not include human beings). They can change how those different forms relate to and affect one another, as in which forms eat which. But the idea of damage and destruction assumes some ideal state, which is primarily a cultural invention. When we forget this—even in trying to 'save' the environment—we make ourselves vulnerable to a kind of species arrogance that, ironically, is also at the root of the environmental damage that so many people (including me) are alarmed about. In other words, it is a kind of arrogance to assume the right to do with the Earth as we please. But it is also a kind of arrogance to assume the right to define what is or is not the ideal state of nature that should be preserved. In either case, we impose human values on a nonhuman world, usually without knowing it.

This does not mean that we shouldn't act on those values. As social beings, we have to act in relation to *some* values, whatever they may be. But it does mean that those on every side of environmental issues may have more in common with one another than they realize, and face similar challenges in understanding their underlying assumptions about what they're doing. It is easy to forget that values are cultural and therefore human and not necessarily reflective of the rest of nature. And in such forgetting, we may speak and act with a sense of righteous authority—whether in defense of jobs and human superiority or the sanctity of ancient forests—that can make all sides sound disturbingly alike.

Making a Living

Every species of life occupies what ecologists call a 'niche' in an ecosystem. A niche is a position, analogous to a status people occupy in a social system. As such, a niche locates a species in relation to a physical environment, other species, and the ecosystem as a whole. Where a species is located in the food chain—what it eats and what eats it—is an important aspect of its ecological niche, as are other practices, such as burrowing holes in the Earth or building dams in streams.

Through its niche, each species lives by using its environment in particular ways. This is as true for humans as for any other species. Hunter-gatherer societies, for example, use minimal technology and produce none of their own food. Horticultural societies grow food in small gardens by using sticks to make holes in the ground for seeds. Agricultural societies use plows and draft animals to cultivate large fields. Industrial societies focus less on contact with raw materials—growing food, mining, lumbering—and more on manufacturing goods from them, especially through the use of machines. In postindustrial societies, providing such services as health care, insurance, banking, and entertainment outweighs producing goods.

To understand human ways of making a living, we need to expand the concept of a niche to include the social relationships that organize productive work. In other words, we need to look at what Marx calls the mode of production. In hunter-gatherer societies, people produce goods in ways that require cooperation, communal effort, and sharing. Capitalist industrial societies, however, are highly competitive and wealth is distributed in very lopsided ways. In horticultural societies, people own the tools and other means of production they use to produce a living, but in industrial capitalist societies, the elite own most means of production but do not personally use them to produce anything. Production is done by workers who make goods in exchange for wages without owning or controlling any part of the process. Such relationships—among people and between people and the means of production—tell us a lot about how the mode of production is organized in a society and how this affects the people who participate in it.

Since the results of production are wealth and what people need to live, how production is organized is especially important in shaping patterns of privilege and oppression. As we look at the historical progression from hunter-gatherer societies to horticulture, agriculture, and industrial capitalism, systematic inequality emerges and grows, beginning with male privilege and the subordination of women. Then come social classes and other patterns in the service of inequality of wealth and power: warfare, conquest, empire, the state, colonialism, institutionalized slavery and racism, and modern class systems and global inequality based on economic power.

In the simplest sense, inequality becomes possible when people are able to produce a surplus that can support larger populations and that enables more and more people to do something other than grow, gather, or hunt for food.[7] This also makes it possible for some to accumulate wealth and power at the expense of others and to defend their position with armies, police, servants, and such institutions as religion and the law, whose purpose almost always includes legitimizing the status quo and the interests of dominant groups.

Historically, none of these patterns of inequality *had* to emerge as a result of increased production, but they could not happen without it. Hunter-gatherer societies, for example, have very low levels of inequality based only on prestige, with honor going to those who perform important jobs well. Inequality cannot be based on wealth in such societies, because they do not produce enough to accumulate and because survival requires a degree of sharing and cooperation that discourages competition and hoarding. They also have to move around so much in search of new food sources that it doesn't make much sense to accumulate things they then have to bring along.

Changes in the mode of production are important because they create conditions that make other social changes more or less likely to occur. The ability to produce a surplus makes rapid population growth, urbanization, and increasingly complex divisions of labor possible. These changes, in turn, make it easier for bureaucracy to emerge as a way to control the system. Historically, bureaucracy emerged in the West along with the capitalist Industrial Revolution, especially in the nineteenth century. But that isn't the only way it came into being. China, for example, has only recently begun to industrialize, but its government has been heavily bureaucratic for centuries. And although the most urbanized societies are industrial, many nonindustrial societies, such as India, Mexico, and Egypt, have experienced an explosion of urban population growth.

Birth, Death, Migration: Population and Social Life

Since every social system happens only when people participate in it, to understand how social life works, we have to pay attention to how many people there are, how they get there, and how and when they leave. Birth and migration are the two ways people enter a society, a family, or a religion, for example, but migration is the only way to enter a workplace or a school (with few exceptions—such as kings and queens or the old Indian caste system or slavery in the United States—no one is born into a job). Too few people in a system can be just as much a problem as too many, as can having the wrong number in the wrong place at the wrong time (as anyone who has been laid off from a job knows).

How big a population is and how fast it grows or shrinks depend on a simple process of addition through births and in-migration and subtraction through deaths and out-migration. In most industrial societies today, births are nearly balanced by deaths, and growth happens primarily through migration. In the United States, migration accounted for just 12 percent of population growth in 1950, compared with 40 percent in 2012. The flow of undocumented immigrants has grown so rapidly that no one really knows just how many people cross the border each year.[8] As of 2012, non-Hispanic white people constituted numerical minorities in the populations of Hawaii, Texas, New Mexico, and California, and the populations of New York, Maryland, Mississippi, Arizona, Nevada, and Georgia were not far behind.[9] Such trends have inspired intense debate over laws to control immigration into the United States and to many parts of Europe—including Britain, France, and Germany—where competition between foreign-born and native-born workers has prompted calls for the expulsion of immigrants.

In nonindustrial societies, which include most of the world, most growth occurs through a surplus of births over deaths. Current growth rates vary from highs of almost 4 percent in Niger to negative rates in Germany and Russia.[10] Four percent may seem like a small number, but not when figured into the law of compound interest. At a 4 percent rate of increase, a population will double in around eighteen years, quadruple in just thirty-five years, and increase *eight-fold* in seventy years, which is less than the average human life span. The world's population is currently growing at a rate of about 1.2 percent per year, which implies a doubling from its current size of around 6 billion people to roughly 12 billion by 2065.

Population affects systems of all kinds and sizes, from households to the world economy. New households and families, for example, are created first through migration when people marry or otherwise decide to move in and live together. In some cultures, the husband is required to move near the wife's family, while in others the pattern is just the opposite. In the latter case, the wife's already-subordinate status in the marriage is reinforced by her physical isolation from kin who might otherwise support her, while in the former, the husband's dominance is lessened by the nearness of the wife's family. In societies where couples can live wherever they want, the problem is more likely to be a lack of contact and support from either family and the kind of isolation characteristic of the modern nuclear family.

The typical new family household starts with a population of two, which is a relatively simple and manageable number. The best way to see this is to imagine what happens when we add just one more to make it three. As we saw in the previous chapter, if the new member is a baby, the structural consequence is a radical change in the household's role structure. But from a population point of view, something else happens as well. With three people, coalitions become possible, as two can gang up against or exclude the third. With just two people, neither can feel excluded, because one person can't create a relationship to exclude the other from. With three people, however, two can form a subgroup within the larger group.

Add a fourth member and it becomes possible to have two subgroups, such as the children and the parents, and thereby two coalitions can shape the distribution of power. Theoretically, children could organize to counter the power of their parents, but it is more likely that one of the children will join with one or both parents to gain power in relation to the other child or parent. Whatever happens structurally, the range of possibilities will vary with the number of people.

As families age, population continues to shape and reshape their culture and structure. As everyone gets older, for example, the age structure shifts upward, and with it may come profound changes in how the family works. Parents lose power as children gain autonomy and independence, and everyone's role expectations begin to change. When children migrate away to go to college or work or to form households of their own, the shift in family power structures becomes even more pronounced, although financial dependence can preserve some aspects of it for a while. In fact, getting out from under parental authority is a major reason why young adult children may long to migrate away and be out on their own.

Physical separation also changes the communication and role structures and may prompt the 'empty nest' syndrome, which can occasion as much relief as grief. If daughters and sons form families of their own, the addition of new members to the network of extended kin increases the overall family population and complicates most of its structural and cultural characteristics. At the other end of the life span, death brings not only loss and grief but also structural and cultural shifts. When our parents die, we can find ourselves feeling as though now we are the true adults in the family with no one in front of us to watch and measure ourselves by. This can be a time of shifting weight in family roles as we step into a sense of responsibility that we would find hard to imagine while our parents were alive.

Such changes flow from the fact that how family life unfolds depends greatly on the dynamics of population through which people are added and subtracted, age, and move around in relation to one another. This dynamic operates in societies and the world as a whole and includes patterns of birth and death that reflect how birthing and dying always happen in relation to social systems.

Although everyone has to die sometime, for example, the statuses we occupy affect how long we're likely to live and our most likely cause of death. Men are consistently more likely than women to die at any given age and from most causes of death. Some of this is undoubtedly due to biological factors, since males are also more likely to die before they're born. But a great deal of the sex differential in death is about sex as a social status. Men are far more likely than women to die from homicide, suicide, and accidents as well as from physical causes, such as cancer and heart disease, that have clear links to how people live. Men are more likely than women to work at hazardous occupations, take physical risks, and act out aggressively. Men are also less likely than women to see a doctor when they're not feeling well, which means they are less likely to discover a life-threatening condition in time to do something about it. They are also heavier users of cigarettes, alcohol, and addictive drugs.[11]

Death and dying have an especially powerful structural connection through the effects of social class and race. The wealthier people are, for example, the more likely they are to describe themselves as being in excellent health, a pattern that repeats itself with educational attainment and occupational prestige.[12] Death rates at each age of life are lowest among those with the most education and highest income. In comparison with white people, the age-adjusted death rate for African Americans is 30 percent higher, the infant mortality rate is more than twice as high, and life expectancy at birth is five years shorter. For homicide, African American death rates are almost six times higher than for white people. Suicide is the only major cause of death with lower rates among African Americans than among white people.[13]

None of these differences tells us what will happen to any specific person who participates in this society, but they do reflect paths of least resistance that load the odds in different ways, depending on our social characteristics. Being a white man doesn't mean that I will someday kill myself, but it does mean that my position in the world makes suicide far more likely for me than for people of color and white women. It also means that I am far less likely to find myself in a situation where I'm likely to be murdered than I would be if I were black. Being in the middle class means being far less likely to work in a dangerous occupation, such as lumbering, trucking, mining, or construction, or to be exposed to cancer-causing chemicals and other threats to health. It also means being less likely to smoke cigarettes or abuse alcohol and more likely to have health insurance and access to quality health care.

If we look at these differences from an individualistic perspective, we might conclude that they are simply a matter of personal choice, as in choosing whether to smoke cigarettes. But applying the basic principle of sociological practice leads straight to the fact that every choice is made in relation to the systems we participate in. From there we have to ask how the paths of least resistance presented to people differ depending on what those systems are and the social positions people occupy in them. In my middle-class neighborhood, there are no billboards with glossy cigarette advertisements, but for many years in inner-city neighborhoods across the United States, cigarette manufacturers have targeted lower- and working-class African Americans with ads that aggressively promote cigarette smoking as a glamorous and attractive thing to do, as one 'pleasure' that is available even to people living in poverty. The path that is easier to follow—to smoke or not to smoke—depends to some extent on where you live, and where you live is invariably affected by social class and race.

Population and the Big Picture

If we look at population at the level of societies or the world as a whole, it is hard to miss the huge and growing mismatch between the needs and resources of societies on the one hand and the size and growth of populations on the other. The fifteen poorest countries of the world contain roughly half the world's population, and countries whose populations account for 80 percent of all the people in the world share less than a quarter of global annual income. In many countries, per-capita income levels have actually fallen in recent years, and recurring periods of famine have become almost permanent facts of life. This will only become worse with the effects of global warming.[14]

A common explanation for the widening gap between rich and poor nations is large differences in birth and growth rates. It is argued that such countries as India, Mexico, and many in Africa, contain too many people. The populations in those countries are growing too rapidly to keep up with the demand for basic services and resources, such as food and water. With Mexico's population growing at a rate of 1.5 percent each year, for example, the economy must also grow 1.5 percent just to keep up, let alone having anything left over to improve standards of living.[15] Since a 1.5 percent rate of economic growth is hard to achieve year after year, it would seem that high rates of population growth virtually ensure continued deprivation and misery for people in Mexico and in many other areas of the world.

What makes a bad situation worse is that high birth rates also result in a high percentage of children in the population, and children are relatively unproductive and claim resources that could otherwise be invested in economic growth. Also making matters worse are migration patterns that swell already-crowded cities, such as Mexico City and Mumbai, India, with unskilled workers looking for relief from rural poverty. What they find, however, is a lack of sanitation, water, food, jobs, and shelter.

The situation in such countries is so dire that it might seem obvious that population would be the most important determining factor in social life. But it's not that simple, because what we call 'overpopulation' is not just a matter of resources' being inadequate *because* there are too many people. Resources can also be inadequate because they are distributed in a way that gives a great deal to some and very little to others.

India, for example, contains 17 percent of all the people in the world but consumes only 5 percent of all the energy used each year. By comparison, the United States has less than 5 percent of the world's population but claims a 19 percent share of all the energy consumed.[16] Which society, then, places a greater burden on the world? Which country shows the greater mismatch between population and resources? Is it India, with its 1.1 billion people, each of whom consumes relatively little? Is it the United States, with only a quarter as many people but who consume almost four times as much? Or is it both?

If we look at the world as a social system, we can ask how population dynamics affect structural patterns of inequality between societies through which resources and wealth are distributed. It might be that there simply is not enough wealth to go around. But it also might be that there is plenty of wealth that is kept from going around by a world system in which enormous economic and political power is held by elites in a tiny number of nations containing a small fraction of the world's people.

Certainly there are practical limits to population growth and size. The human species—within societies and in the world as a whole—cannot indefinitely ignore the natural laws that limit the populations of every other form of life. But it would seem equally clear that wealthy countries cannot continue indefinitely to pretend that population is the only or even the primary issue shaping the fate of nonindustrial societies and that the solution to the misery of billions of people is simply for there to be fewer of them. The principle that we are always participating in something larger than ourselves applies as much to nations as it does to individuals. In that sense, the wealth of the industrial world and the pervasive poverty found everywhere else are connected to each other, and sociological practice is a powerful way to see just how this happens and why it matters.

5

Us, It, and Social Interaction

Having spent four chapters on social systems, those things larger than ourselves that we participate in, it's time to look more closely at the 'we' and what our participation is all about. Social systems do not happen without us, and, in important ways, we do not happen without them. On the one hand, systems contain paths of least resistance, but we are the ones who perceive, interpret, and choose among those paths. We make visible and manifest whatever power they have to shape social life. On the other hand, we live as thinking, acting beings, and yet the stuff that thoughts are made of and the meaning of our actions make sense only in relation to cultural, structural, and ecological aspects of social systems.

Self: The I Who Participates

"Take care of yourself," a friend of mine says at the end of a conversation. As I return to this work, I wonder just what that means. Who or what is this self I'm supposed to take care of, and is the 'I' who takes care of that self something other than the self that gets taken care of? Is my self something I can touch, hear, or smell? I can sense my body and what it does, but my self is more than that.

Behavioral psychologists, such as B. F. Skinner, have little interest in the self, since they cannot figure out a way to observe it scientifically.[1] And yet we think about the self as something real and thinglike that is responsible for what we do. When my 'body' does something wrong—as when my hand takes something that doesn't belong to me—no one blames my body, even though it did the deed. Nor do they blame my brain ("Bad brain!"), which directed my body to do it. They blame my self ("*You* should be ashamed of yourself"). What that self is that I'm supposed to be ashamed of and where I am likely to find it are elusive things, because more than anything, the self is an *idea* we have about our own existence.[2] But it is a powerful idea, because we do not live it as such: we act as though the self is as real as anything we can see and touch.

Part of what makes the idea of the self so powerful is that it locates us in relation to other people and social systems. One answer to the question, 'Who am I?' is 'Allan Griswold Johnson,' three words that name me in the same way that words name an oak tree or a banana. They also serve a similar purpose. In my culture, they identify me as male (Allan being regarded as a man's name) and thereby distinguish me from females. They distinguish me from all the people I am not (except for those who have the same name). And they connect me to kin marked by common names—Griswold being my mother's family name and Johnson my father's. A person's name, then, and the self that it names have a purely *relational* purpose of marking us in relation to others. The only reason to have a name is to be able to participate in social life, and this is also why we develop ideas about the self in general and about our own selves in particular.

As philosopher and sociologist George Herbert Mead sees it, we discover ourselves as children through a process of discovering others and the ideas they have about themselves and about us.[3] Infants tend to experience the world in an egocentric way in that they cannot distinguish between the world and themselves. Everything is just one big whole, with them at the center of it all. This leaves them without a way to know that other people exist as separate people with thoughts and feelings. As an infant, I could not imagine that my mother had a point of view on things, including me. I could not see that she thought about herself in relation to me and me in relation to her or about things that had to do with neither at all. I could feel her body and otherwise sense what she did and said, but I had no way to know there was something going on beneath all that, that she had ideas about who she was or who I was or about how to be a good mother or what kind of man I would grow up to be or what to have for dinner.

If I could not imagine that my mother had a point of view on herself and the world, then I also could not imagine that I had a point of view on anything. As far as I could tell, the way I heard and felt and otherwise sensed things was simply the way things were and had nothing to do with who I was in relation to them or how I perceived or interpreted them. I was like a baseball umpire who, instead of saying, "I call 'em as I see 'em" or (confidently) "I call 'em as they *are*," says, "*Until* I call 'em, they *aren't*."

As an infant, I could not be aware that I had a point of view on things, because I had no way to *think* about myself *as* a self, to imagine an 'Allan' who existed in the first place. Mead argues that we learn to think about ourselves as selves by discovering the inner lives of other people. We realize that other people think about us, perceive us in certain ways, expect things of us, have feelings about us, and have lives separate from our own that in many ways have nothing to do with us. This happens primarily when people use language to talk about themselves, us, and what *they* experience as reality. They use language as a bridge of meaning to connect their experience to the experiences of other people. When I was hungry, I might have experienced that as just a bodily discomfort, an empty feeling in my stomach that made me cry until it was taken care of. But when someone used words like 'I'm hungry' to describe that experience, then I could imagine how they felt and put myself in their place.

Without language, Mead argues, there is no way to be aware of that otherwise invisible realm known as the self, and without that, children have no way to construct their own ideas about who they are *as* selves. It is through language, then, that we discover the human *possibility* of a self by discovering what other people have done with that possibility. We become aware of our point of view *as* a point of view rather than as 'the way things are.'

Once we see this, we can construct all kinds of ideas about ourselves that make up the self. Because they are *about* the self, we use them to think about the self just as we would think about someone else (as in 'how to be your own best friend'). We can talk to it, have feelings about it, evaluate and judge it, believe in it or not, defend or condemn it, scold or praise it, feel proud or ashamed of it, 'get hold' of it, disown it ('I'm not myself today'), lose it, be conscious of it ('self-conscious') or not, or try to accept, understand, or 'get over' it. We can say and do things to affect how other people perceive us and how they treat us as a result. We can wade into deep pools of paradox, thinking of ourselves as unique and separate from the world around us, even though 'unique' is a cultural concept from that same world, and the self exists only in relation to other selves.

No wonder one of our most exhilarating experiences is when someone 'believes' in us. And no wonder one of the greatest crises we can experience happens when we stop 'believing in ourselves' and feel lost, cut loose with nothing to hang onto.

Note, however, that whether this experience turns into a crisis depends on the culture we live in. In many Asian cultures, thinking of the self as unique and separate from groups and society is neither a given nor an ideal of social life. In traditional Japanese culture, for example, it is a far greater crisis to lose a deep sense of attachment to the whole and be thrust from it into the uncertainties of the individual self.

To participate as selves in social systems, we have to locate ourselves in relation to them by seeing how and where we connect to them and how this reflects back a sense of who we are. Most people do not know that self my friend told me to take care of. What they do know about me are the statuses I occupy and the roles that go with them. At birth, we are known only by a handful of statuses—gender, race, age, and family position—because there is not much else about us to know. As we grow, we accumulate a social identity by occupying one status after another and using them to locate ourselves in relation to social systems and other people.

As Erving Goffman points out, when we occupy a status, the role that goes with it provides us with a ready-made self that we can adopt as a path of least resistance toward acceptance by others.[4] In this sense, most people know little about who we are on the inside. What they 'know' consists primarily of cultural images of the typical person who occupies this or that status—the typical girl, the typical student, the typical lawyer, the typical business manager, the typical politician. In social space, we are not 'who we are' in some absolute, objective sense. We are who people *think* we are, a reality they construct from cultural ideas before they know anything about us based on direct experience.

Most people, for example, know very little about the real me as I experience myself. But anyone who thinks they know about fathers, men, heterosexuals, white people, writers, grandfathers, brothers, husbands, public speakers, baby boomers, Ph.D. recipients, the middle class, and people whose households include dogs, goats, and a snake may think they know quite a lot about me. What they actually know, however, are paths of least resistance that go with statuses I occupy and the likelihood that I usually follow those paths. I may, in fact, choose quite differently, but they can't know that unless they see how I participate in social life.

Not only do other people know us primarily through role relationships, but this is also a major way for us to know ourselves. Think back for a moment to Mead's idea that we discover ourselves through first discovering others. If so, then it follows that how we see, evaluate, and feel about ourselves is shaped by the statuses we occupy, which means that as we construct the ideas and feelings about who we are that constitute the social self, we depend primarily on information that comes from outside ourselves.

These outside sources of information take the form of two kinds of 'others.' Significant others are specific people who act like mirrors, reflecting images back to us that we may incorporate into our sense of who we are.[5] 'Significant' in this case means 'specific' rather than important. If a man in the audience at one of my presentations comes up to me afterward and tells me he thinks I did a great job (or a rotten one), he becomes a significant other for me, because the information he gives comes from him as an individual. He also offers me a reflection of myself to consider as information that I may or may not include in my sense of who I am. This reflection is known as the 'looking-glass self': I use him as a mirror, and the reflection consists of what I *think* he thinks of me (which may or may not turn out to match how he actually sees me).[6]

Early in life, most information about ourselves comes from significant others, such as family members and playmates. Only later through a complex process of socialization do we begin to grasp what is called the 'generalized other.'[7] The generalized other is not a specific person or even a group of people. It is our *perception* of how people in *general* view a social situation and the people who occupy different statuses within it.

When I go to my regular dentist, David, for a checkup, for example, I interact with someone I know as an individual. I know something about what he expects, what he's like as a person, and how he does things. This makes him a significant other to me. When I went to him for the first time, however, his name, gender, race, approximate age, and occupation were the only things I knew about him as an individual. How, then, did I know how to behave, and how did he? Without knowing each other, we had to rely on cultural ideas about dentists and their patients and what goes on between them. Until we learned about each other as significant others, these generalized others were all we had to put together some idea of what the *situation* was about and who he and I were in relation to each other. In the beginning, we knew only the statuses we occupied and the social relationship between them. In other words, we knew each 'other' only in a generalized way.

What makes the generalized other difficult for young children to grasp is that it's a purely abstract collection of ideas about status occupants. We learn what significant others expect from us by what they say and do, and children pick that up very quickly. But to distinguish between the specific woman who is my mother and 'mother' as a social status requires a level of cognitive ability that develops only as children mature.

The ideas that make up the generalized other are cultural, which encourages us to assume that we share their meanings with other people. On the basis of this belief, we also assume that people will perceive, interpret, and evaluate us in certain ways when they know which statuses we occupy. This is why people who are lesbian, gay, or bisexual may tend to be careful about revealing their sexual orientation to heterosexuals. It is also why heterosexuals feel no qualms at all about revealing theirs, to the extent that they do not experience it as revealing something at all, much less coming out or 'admitting' their sexual orientation. It is why it matters what clothes we wear when we go out in public, especially how we present ourselves as male or female, because such choices shape who other people think we are. This is why privilege and oppression based on race, gender, and disability status are so powerful. People think they know which status we occupy simply by looking at us or even just hearing our names, and, as a result, easily associate us with ideas about who we are, whether we are 'normal,' what we can and cannot do, what we are worth, and what our rights are in relation to them. In this sense, we need to extend the idea that we construct reality in a cultural sense (introduced in Chapter 2), for the reality we create is also profoundly structural in relation to statuses, roles, and the generalized other.

Since statuses and roles are elements of social systems, who we are—to ourselves and to other people—is profoundly rooted in our participation in systems and the socialization process through which we learn how to do it. This makes understanding ourselves a basic part of sociological practice and not merely the province of psychology. Statuses and roles connect us to the social world and overlap our lives with other people's lives. They locate, identify, and anchor us in social space. Without them, we do not exist in a social sense, and without that, there is little left of what we know and experience as a self or a life.

This can be a disturbing idea for people living in a culture that places a high value on being an autonomous and unique individual. But, in fact, it does not diminish our worth as people. It simply means that we (and our worth) exist in relation to something larger, that we are not the beginning and end of things. Even rebels and iconoclasts who reject society are organizing their sense of self and their lives in relation to something larger than themselves—the society they reject. And they occupy recognizable statuses within those societies, such as 'rebel' and 'iconoclast.' In most high schools and colleges, for example, a few students usually play the role of the 'nonconformist' who conforms to a cultural type by openly rejecting the idea of conforming to cultural types.

None of this means that we are nothing more than occupants of statuses and roles. Not only can we make creative choices about how to participate in social systems, but there are mysteries of human existence that are far more than social constructions. Every culture has *ideas* about such mysteries and about itself, but the best we can do with them is to construct reality second- or third-hand. Only in rare moments do we manage to shake ourselves loose from social systems and experience the mysteries of life and death more directly. But that experience can be enough to remind us that however we construct our sense of social life and ourselves, mystery piled upon mystery lie beneath it. We are not machines, and neither are social systems. Both are far more complex, elusive, and interesting than that.

Self in Systems

The key to how we participate in systems is the concept of social interaction, and the key to that is the difference between action and behavior. Everything we do is behavior, but only some behavior takes the form of action.

A baby girl's first step, for example, is a behavior but not an action. When she is older and walks across the room in response to someone saying, "Please come here," however, what she is doing is both a behavior and an action. The difference? In the first case, the behavior involves no interpretation on her part. She does not consider the meaning of what she is doing (and not doing) and how this behavior will be perceived and interpreted by someone else. She does not consider it because she lacks the language and abstract cultural ideas necessary for thinking about what she is doing or what other people expect of her and make of what she does. In the second case, she can use language to anticipate what her behavior would mean to someone else and then take this idea into account in choosing what to do. She can imagine alternatives and the most likely responses to each.

In short, behavior based on meaning is action, and actions are the building blocks of our participation in social systems and social life as we interact with other people.

On the level of individuals, interaction is the process through which social systems happen, but it is also how *we* happen as social beings. As Goffman puts it in several fascinating books, we are like actors on a stage.[8] Every social situation has its props and setting, its script and opportunities for improvisation. And every play has an audience, except that in social life we are all actors and part of someone else's audience at the same time.

As actors, we use a variety of techniques to have our performances seen as authentic, as worthy of the role we are playing, as being convincing enough for us to be accepted in that situation for who we claim to be. We usually make an effort to show up looking the part, for example, and wearing the right clothes, having the right attitude for the situation, knowing our lines, and carrying the right props. Like actors, we create impressions of who we are, what Goffman calls 'the presentation of self.'

Like every impression, the presentation of self is an ongoing process. It needs to be sustained and managed, especially when we do something that is 'out of character' or otherwise calls our performance into question. When two people go out on a date, for example, each spends time shaping the self they will present to the other—choosing what to wear, whether to shower or use deodorant or cologne, how to style their hair, the use of jewelry and makeup. Every action contributes to the impression they create—what they say and how they say it, what they order in the restaurant and how they eat it, when, how often, and how long they look at each other, and with what facial expression, what they laugh at and what they don't, how much they talk and how much they listen, and how and when they touch each other.

When they part company, each is likely to wonder about the impression made on the other, whether they said or did something that was misunderstood, taken to indicate something about the self that doesn't fit with how they see themselves or would like to be seen. Like players before an audience, as the curtain falls, they wait for the response, the volume and duration of applause, anything that might tell them how well their performance was accepted. On a date, it might be whether a kiss goodnight is forthcoming, or whether the "I had a great time" or "I'll call you" sounds sincere or merely polite (yet another way to manage impressions).

As in a play, both actors and audience in social life want everything to go as it's supposed to, because if it does not, it may compromise our own ability to play our roles effectively. Even as an audience for someone else's performance, we are never just that, for the audience has its role to play, too. This is why when actors in a theater forget their lines or otherwise ruin their performances, people in the audience often feel uncomfortable. The role of witness to someone else's failed performance is difficult to play, because the mere fact of our sitting there and watching it happen contributes to the actor's pain. We become part of the actor's failure, since if we were not there— if there were no audience—the failure could not happen.

And so we do what we can to protect the actor from failure. We don't call attention to the forgotten line, the stumble, the momentary lapse, the wooden delivery, but act as though it never happened, allowing the performance to continue with the hope that the people 'on stage' will 'get their act together.' In doing this, we protect them and ourselves as well as the integrity of the play in which we all participate. Both actors and audience have impressions to manage.

As actors, of course, there are many things we can do to protect our own performances. We can disown them with such disclaimers as "I was only kidding" or "I didn't mean it" or "I don't know what came over me." A man might say something sexist but then try to distance himself from it by saying that it doesn't mean that *he* is sexist. Or, as Goffman points out, he might react with embarrassment that lets people know that although his performance may have failed this time, he is still committed to doing better the next time around.[9] His red face and awkwardness show that he believes in the importance of what people expect of him, a display that may protect him by reinforcing his claim to the part he has in the play.

Looking at social life as theater might give us reason to wonder whether we have an authentic self at all, whether everything isn't just a cynical matter of figuring out how to make the best impression, protect performances, and play audience to someone else. The very idea of a role can seem to preclude the possibility of being authentic, as if creating impressions and trying to turn in an acceptable performance invariably mean faking it and wearing masks that conceal our 'real' selves.

But the line between who we are and how we participate in social life is not as clear and neat as it might seem. To act as though it were is to invite all kinds of trouble. If we pretend that our role behavior is somehow not connected to who we really are, for example, then we avoid taking responsibility not only for the role but also for our portion of the play.

Goffman argues that we are always being ourselves, even though we may feel uncomfortable owning up to the results and allowing them to affect how other people see us. If I play a role in a way that seems to contradict who I think I am, the person playing that role is still me and is no less real than the 'me' who rejects this performance as not reflecting the real me. If I fake it and act in ways that don't reflect how I really feel, it is still me who does the faking, who appears and behaves in ways that create a particular impression.

Whatever the performance turns out to be, it comes from somewhere in me, and any unreality in that lies in my not being aware of it and denying my connection to the consequences my behavior produces. As such, the problem of authenticity is not that we perform roles and manage impressions. The problem is that we don't embrace and own our actions for what they are as part of *who* we are. The problem is not that we have so many roles to perform that can make us appear inconsistent or other than we'd like. The problem is that we do not integrate them with an ongoing awareness of the incredible complexity of ourselves and the social life in which we participate.

Not seeing this complexity sets us up to participate unknowingly in systems that produce all kinds of consequences, both good and bad. At the same time, we cut ourselves off from our potential to do something about consequences we want to change. When white people act in racist ways, for example, they often rush to make the point that they are not themselves racist. "I didn't mean it," they say, or "I misspoke," or "I made a mistake [by saying that], and I'm sorry." They almost never respond with something like, "I guess the racism in the world gets into all of our lives, including mine, and I'd better look at that to see what that means for me."

In terms of impression management, everything said in self-defense is probably true: they did not *intend* to say or do anything that would hurt someone or add racism to the impression people have of them. But this is beside the more important point that the racist content of social action is real, and if people choose—consciously or not—to be vehicles for its expression, this says something about the systems they participate in *and* about them as participants. In a racist society, talk and action that reflect and reinforce white privilege are paths of least resistance that tell us more about society than about ourselves. But the choices we make in relation to those paths tell us something about who we are in relation to them, and if we don't see that, we cannot do anything about the paths or about ourselves.

Few things in sociological practice are as important or as tricky to grasp as the relationship between people and systems. In an individualistic society, the path of least resistance is to ignore systems altogether or to see them as vague menacing forces that threaten to swallow us up. The truth, however, is more complicated than that, and with far more potential for creative living.

Our relationship to a system's culture, for example, is dynamic and alive, with us creating the world as much as we are created by and through it. We are objects of culture—described, valued, and limited by its ideas about who we are and how we ought to think, feel, and behave. We are also subjects of culture, the ones who believe, who value, who expect, who feel, who use, who write and talk and think and dream. We are creators of culture, part of an endless stream of human experience—sensing, interpreting, choosing, shaping, making. We are the ones who make culture our own so that we often can't tell the point where it leaves off and we begin, or whether that point exists at all. We are recipients of culture, socialized and enculturated. We are the ones who internalize ideas, taking them inside ourselves where they shape how we participate in social life and thereby make it happen. And this thing we make happen is at the same time the cultural force that shapes us as *we* happen.

As a creative medium that we share with others, culture is not us, but it also is not completely external to us. It exists through us as we exist through it. It is *among* and *of* us. Our participation in it provides a way to participate in other people's lives. In this sense, there is no clear, fixed boundary that separates us from culture and, therefore, no clear, fixed boundary that separates us from other people. Culture is like the air. It is everywhere, and as humans we cannot live without it. We can live without any particular culture, but not without *some* culture.

Like the air, culture flows in and out of us in ways that make it impossible to draw a true line between 'I' or 'us' and 'it.' The air is both outside us and inside every cell of our bodies. As beings, we are of the air, but in a particular form that distinguishes us from dogs or ferns or bacteria. And since we all share this relationship with the air—as with culture—in a way we are all of one another. You are part of flowing and mixing with the same air that inhabits me.

Culture provides ideas and materials to work with as we make ourselves and social life happen from one moment to the next, but we have to decide what to do with them. Culture isn't something that can think or decide or do anything, nor is any other aspect of social systems or the systems themselves. We are not autonomous and independent in relation to systems, but we also aren't puppets on a string. We are somewhere in between in a far more creative place.

We're like jazz improvisers who cannot play without learning the basics of music. They have to know the difference between a sharp and a flat and between major and minor and how notes combine to make different kinds of chords. They have to know how to blend time, rhythm, and sound so they can shape the flow of the music and stay in sync while they play together. In other words, they need to know how symbols and ideas define and underlie jazz as a musical form and how they shape the way musicians think, hear, imagine, and relate to one another in ways both structural and ecological. But the social forms that limit them are also what they use to create, to bend and play with the 'rules,' to test the limits in ways that sound both familiar ('music,' 'jazz') and new, what it means to improvise.

This doesn't mean they can do whatever they want, even though jazz can sound that way, as if everyone is doing their own thing oblivious to everyone else. In fact, however, they are deeply aware of one another and the form within which they play all the while they're making it up as they go along. Beneath the seeming creative disorder lies an unarticulated inner discipline based on their shared participation in a social system. This is what gives the entire piece its musical integrity and its *social* integrity as something happening not merely *within* individual musicians but also *among* them. This ability to play within a form and yet improvise around and, at times, beyond it is what gives jazz its unmistakable character. As with jazz and its musicians, so also with social life and us.

Making Systems Happen

Social interaction consists of all the ways that we create and sustain a particular sense of reality out of which our lives, systems, and social life happen. Social interaction is the interplay between us and systems that works through both action and appearance. If employees in a bank, for example, dress in clown costumes and gorilla suits, customers will have a hard time identifying the bank as a company where they can confidently deposit their money. Appearance and action mirror each other. The hushed atmosphere in a typical bank and the quiet, efficient way that tellers handle transactions sustain the shared sense that this is a serious place where your money will be well taken care of. People don't laugh a lot in banks or make jokes about bank failures or embezzlement, just as airline pilots and flight attendants don't make funny remarks about crashes or bombs.

In fact, in the United States, especially since the events of September 11, 2001, you run the risk of being arrested for making jokes in an airport about possibly carrying a bomb onto a plane. This policy exists because the shared sense that flying is a safe way to travel is a fragile social reality even without the threat of terrorism and it can be sustained only by controlling anything that people might say or do to indicate otherwise. As I sit in my seat at 30,000 feet, reading a book or listening to music on my iPod, I'm usually unaware of the fine line that separates the alternate realities of safety and imminent danger, and everything around me is designed to encourage me not to. The comfort of the seats, the availability of movies, food, reading material, music, air-conditioning, heat, Wi-Fi, and phones—all create a sense of reality that, when I consider where it is taking place, is in some ways absurd. But I accept the situation and make it 'normal' and unremarkable in my mind until something happens to suggest otherwise.

Every social situation is defined by a reality that exists only as people actively shape and support it.[10] In something as simple as a conversation, we have to engage in a kind of dance of gestures, talk, and body language to sustain a shared sense that this thing we call a conversation is, in fact, happening from one moment to the next. We can use all kinds of methods, for example, to assure people that we are paying attention to what they're saying. We look at them, nod our heads now and then, murmur an occasional "uh-huh," smile or laugh at the funny parts, frown at something serious, ask a question or make a comment that's related to what they said. Without that assurance, the idea that a conversation is happening cannot be sustained as a shared reality.

A workshop exercise makes this point come alive. People pair off and one person tells a story to the other while the partner pretends to be completely oblivious to what's being said (sometimes going to sleep). It's an awful experience for the speakers, who typically cannot think of what to say next or can but cannot get their mouths to say it. In this sense, 'having a conversation' is a reality that we create and sustain between us, and everything we do or don't do figures into making it happen. The methods are something we have to learn, and they vary from one system to another.

In some societies, for example, a sign of paying attention in a conversation is looking at the other person's eyes from time to time. In other societies, however, this is considered a sign of disrespect if done by someone lower in authority toward someone higher. So, when typical middle-class white teachers in U.S. schools try to have a conversation with students from any number of Latin American or Asian societies, they find their students seeming to shirk their responsibility to help keep the conversation going (thinking, perhaps, the students are trying to conceal some wrongdoing), when what is really going on is a show of respect and politeness. What sustains a conversation in one system can have just the opposite effect in another.

We continually use our beliefs of how reality is constructed to figure out from one moment to the next what is happening and how to do our part to keep it going. At the movies, for example, I walk up to the theater and notice a line of people extending out the front door and down the sidewalk. I take this to mean that the theater hasn't started selling tickets for the next show and that I'm supposed to go to the end of the line and wait for it to move. The social reality of a waiting line is a fragile one, because most people would rather be at the front than farther back. It is so fragile that the smallest thing can make it come undone. It takes only a few people to leave the line, for example, and go into the door ahead of everyone else for people to start doubting that it is in fact a 'line' in which the rules of staying in place and waiting your turn apply. When this happens, the line can fall apart physically and as a shared social reality, which depends on certain patterns of social action to maintain a consensus that it exists.

Because the methods we use to sustain a social reality are used over and over again, they often take on a ritual quality.[11] Intimate relations between marital partners, for example, are usually based on the assumption that the two people love each other. Since an assumption is just an idea, it is sustained through rituals that call attention to it as part of the reality these two people participate in day after day. Such rituals might include saying, "Good night" before going to sleep, perhaps accompanied with a kiss, or saying, "I love you" before ending a phone conversation, or kissing as part of saying good-bye when going off in separate directions at the start of a day.

We may not think of such rituals as sustaining a reality until our partner fails to enact them, especially over a period of time. In itself, each "I love you," each kiss, each "Good night" does not amount to much, but as part of a fabric that holds together the social reality of a love relationship, it can take on much greater significance. It may not take many lapses to raise insecurity in a partner or worry that something is wrong in the relationship, that the assumption of love and commitment is weaker than it was or may never have been what they thought. Those rituals are like many interaction rituals in that we do not know they are there until someone deviates from them and we notice the hole in the social fabric that marks where they are supposed to be.

Large Structures in Everyday Life

A focus on interaction naturally draws us toward individuals, but it is important to keep in mind that almost everything we say or do happens in relation to one social system or another and often has implications for larger systems, even though we do not know it at the time.

Linguist Deborah Tannen, for example, has written several books on how women and men talk to one another.[12] She notices that men tend to talk in ways that enhance their status—they are more likely than women to interrupt during conversations, use aggressive language and tones of voice, and avoid doing anything that might suggest a lack of control, such as asking for directions or saying they do not know the answer to a question. Women, on the other hand, are more likely than men to interact in ways that support personal relationships—to listen attentively while others talk, wait their turn rather than interrupt, avoid verbal aggression, and be more open about their doubts. Tannen explains these patterns as a relatively simple matter of children playing in same-sex groups as they grow up, thereby socialized by their peers to interact in different ways. They grow up in what amounts to different cultures, Tannen argues, and behave accordingly.

The problem with Tannen's approach is that she never links such differences to the larger social context that makes them paths of least resistance. She tells us, for example, that a boy learns to interact aggressively by hanging out with other boys, but she doesn't say where *those* boys learn to interact aggressively. It's as though boys and girls invent different patterns spontaneously and all by themselves, rather than learning them as part of their socialization into the larger society they *both* inhabit.

More importantly, Tannen doesn't ask what kind of society would have paths of least resistance that lead men to seek status and women to attend to personal relationships. She barely mentions that we live in a society that is male-dominated, male-identified, and male-centered. In such a world, men who seek status and women who tend to personal relationships also reinforce male privilege and the oppressive price that privilege exacts from women.

When women and men interact along paths of least resistance, they do more than talk differently. They also play a part in making a particular kind of society happen from one moment to the next. When men interrupt and women don't object, when men answer questions even when they do not know the answer and women remain silent or say they don't know even when they do, when men argue aggressively for their point of view and women raise questions and otherwise show an openness to alternatives— this is how the system of male privilege *happens* in order to shape a major structural feature of society as a whole and all of the systems, from family to workplace, included in it.

This is true of every form of social inequality, whose patterns of inclusion and exclusion, advantage and disadvantage, reward and punishment contribute to privileging some groups over others. In all kinds of workplaces, for example, white women, people of color, people who are LGBT,* and people with disabilities find themselves on the receiving end of messages that make them feel like unwelcome outsiders. Sometimes these messages are overt and deliberate, but often they are woven into the everyday fabric of interaction.

As Rosabeth Moss Kanter has observed about corporations, for example, when men use strong language in the presence of women, they may make a point of apologizing to the women.[13] While the men may think they are being sensitive or polite, they are also sending the message that without the women there, they wouldn't have to pay such close attention to how they talk. By apologizing, men draw attention to the exceptional nature of women's presence and identify women as outsiders who interfere with what would otherwise be regarded as the normal flow of conversation.

Gays and lesbians experience this kind of exclusion all the time in the

---

*LGBT is an acronym for lesbian, gay, bisexual, and transgender. Some activists expand it to include 'queer' (LGBTQ), a general term that refers to those who, in various ways, reject, test, or otherwise transgress the boundaries of what is culturally regarded as normal with respect to gender, gender identity, or sexual orientation and expression. Some regard it as an umbrella term for the other four components of LGBT. 'Queer,' of course, is also routinely used as an insult directed at LGBT people.

form of an ongoing assumption by heterosexuals that everyone else is heterosexual, too.[14] Since coming out carries all kinds of risks at work, for example, gays and lesbians have to be careful in the simplest everyday interactions, such as Monday morning talk about what coworkers did over the weekend. When heterosexuals try to imagine telling someone all about their family without ever using a word that indicates anyone's gender, they get some idea of what it's like to be gay or lesbian in the typical workplace. A heterosexual has nothing to lose by casually revealing a partner's gender, as when a woman refers to her partner as 'he.' But a lesbian who does the same thing could find herself in trouble, excluded if not harassed and discriminated against in ways that threaten her livelihood. Since heterosexuals have much greater freedom to talk about their personal lives, such talk becomes a form of privilege, because it is denied to others.[15] That heterosexuals are rarely aware of this is also part of their privilege.

In a society that privileges whiteness, people of many races must deal with patterns of interaction that exclude and discriminate. The messages 'You are not white' and 'You don't belong here' are sent in a variety of ways. Black men, for example, are routinely treated as objects of fear in public places, as white people hug packages and bags more tightly against their bodies as they pass by or avoid the encounter by crossing the street. Black people also often have their presence challenged, however politely.

A black partner in a large law firm, for example, came to work early one morning and was confronted by a young newly hired white attorney who did not know whom he was talking to.

"Can I help you?" the young man asked pointedly. When told "No," he repeated the question until the senior lawyer angrily explained who he was.

A black federal judge tells the story of waiting for a cab with several colleagues—all dressed in suits and ties—outside a prominent hotel in a major city. A white woman drove up in her car, got out, and handed the judge her keys as she strode into the hotel.[16]

In such ways, the large structures of social inequality that characterize entire societies play themselves out in everyday life. The countless ways that such systems limit and damage people's lives don't usually take the form of overt and deliberate harm. Instead, they happen through a particular choice of words, a tone of voice, the timing of a silence or an averted gaze, or a seemingly innocent question. Such patterns make it difficult for members of dominant groups to appreciate that their privilege even exists, not to mention the cost that their privilege exacts from others. And those patterns also make it difficult for members of subordinate groups to endure the small everyday exclusions and insults, no single one of which carries great weight but which accumulate into the kind of burden that gives oppression its name.

The interplay between the details of speech, gesture, and behavior on the one hand and how social systems happen on the other operates in some way at every level and in every realm of social life. This interplay gives significance to everything we do and do not do and to the choices that shape how we do it. It is, ultimately, what connects us to a social reality larger than ourselves and our own experience, a reality shaped through our participation, which, at the same time, shapes who we are.

6

Things Are Not
What They Seem

Sociology is not simply a field of study, a discipline, or an intellectual pursuit. It is also a form of practice, a way of living in the world. As such, it can change how we see and experience reality by revealing assumptions and understandings that underlie everyday life. Many of these are rarely spoken or otherwise made explicit, and yet they operate in powerful ways to shape our perceptions, thoughts, feelings, and behavior. By going beneath the surface, sociology reveals a deeper and more complex reality.

This happens on every level of human experience, from global politics to the most intimate relationship. What does it mean, for example, when someone says, "I love you"? Why does it matter so much when the 'wrong' person says it or the 'right' person does not?

Or why do so many people not vote in U.S. elections? In a country that prides itself on its democracy, why does a lower percentage of people vote than almost anywhere else?

Or why is poverty so pervasive and persistent in the wealthiest country in the world? Why do no solutions seem to work?

And why is the fact that most violence is committed by men not identified as a key to understanding the epidemic of violence in the world? What makes men's violence so invisible?

"I Love You"

To most of us, language is little more than a way to label the world, to represent symbolically what we perceive, think, and feel and to communicate it to other people. But as we saw in Chapter 2, it is much more than that. Language is also a shared medium for creating what we take to be reality in each social situation. As such, it acts as a powerful glue that holds social systems and our participation in them together. It allows us to assume basic outlines of what is real and what is not, without which social life could not happen.

Of all the uses of language, one of the most intriguing and least studied is 'performative language,' expressions that count as actions in and of themselves. We often use language to describe what we've done, for example, or what we're doing or intend to do. But while the words have meaning, saying them is not in itself a social action.

I might say, for example, "I've been thinking about quitting my job," but I haven't done anything beyond saying some words to communicate what I think. If I go to my employer, however, and say, "I quit," then I haven't just used words to convey meaning but have also *done* something. I have actually quit my job by saying the words, and in that action I have changed a piece of social reality—my relation to my employer and the social system where I'm employed.

Action is what makes performative language *performative*: the words are not just *about* some aspect of reality but are a meaningful action in and of themselves that *changes* reality. They are an action because the content of what is said is regarded as action beyond the mechanics of talk. In the same way, when I say, "I promise to pay you the money I owe," I do not just communicate my intentions. I also *do* something by saying words that actually change my relationship to the person I'm saying them to. The words invoke a set of social expectations that bind me to certain actions and give others the right to hold me accountable to them. To say, "I promise" *is* to promise and has consequences that are no less concrete than any other social action. This is true for any kind of oath, from swearing to tell the truth in court to swearing loyalty to a government.

Probably the best-known example of performative language is the "I do" spoken by people in the act of getting married. It is no accident that these two simple words are so often a source of tension and humor in movies as the audience waits breathlessly while a character stands there in silence, hesitating, holding onto the potential *not* to say them. All the other words in a marriage ceremony amount to nothing without these two. When spoken at the right moment, they have the social authority to literally transform the relationship between two people and their families and between them and such institutions as the state, whose approval is necessary to undo the effects of saying them.

It is relatively easy to see how the phrases 'I promise,' 'I quit,' and 'I do' qualify as performative language, but a more interesting case is performative language that doesn't stand out quite so clearly. When I say, "I'm sorry," for example, I could simply be expressing sorrow for someone else's loss or pain, regardless of whether I had anything to do with causing it. The words could also serve, however, as performative language that alters my relationship with someone else.

If I hurt people, for example, by being insensitive to their feelings, I incur a social obligation to accept their anger because they are seen as having a right to it. I am also obliged to at least try to make it up to them in some way. One way to escape the anger and the obligation—to return the relationship to the way it was before—is to use 'I'm sorry' as performative language that can get me off the hook. I hurt their feelings, they get angry, and then I say, "I'm sorry." When they persist in feeling angry, I ward them off with, "I said I was sorry, didn't I?" If the words simply expressed my feelings, they would have relatively little effect ("You may feel sorry, but I'm still hurt!"). But as performative language, they can alter the relationship itself if the person no longer feels that they have the right to continue being angry and to hold me to my obligation to do something to make up for the injury I have caused, if only to endure their anger.

This kind of performative language is powerful because we are unaware that it's performative. The phrase 'I love you' is a prime example that may also be the single most potent (and dangerous) bit of hidden performative language there is.

Since the emergence of romantic love in the European age of chivalry, 'I love you' has become one of the most important phrases people hope to hear or have occasion to say. Especially in Western societies (but increasingly elsewhere as well), there seems to be an obsession with love—getting it, having it, keeping it, and recovering from the loss of it. Love is everywhere, from literature and film to music, art, and the corridors of every high school. Few things in our lives seem to have as much power to shape our sense of well-being or our willingness to take risks that might make us look like fools as the quest to hear those three short words spoken by the right person at the right time.

What, then, do the words mean? More importantly, what meaningful action does saying them perform?

In the simplest sense, they work like any other words to convey information, except in this case the information takes on a high cultural value, given what it says about how one person perceives and feels about another. If this were all that 'I love you' was about, then we would all want to hear it as often as possible, especially in a society where people are obsessed with loving and being loved. But this is not the case, for the 'wrong' person saying, "I love you" can be just as much a problem as the 'right' person *not* saying it. Saying (and not saying), "I love you" is so problematic because the words do much more than communicate information about reality. They also play a key performative role in *altering* reality. This is why those three little words are the source of so much attention and trouble.

We could, for example, see 'I love you' as a gift or a compliment. If we follow the norm of reciprocity,[1] we feel obliged to complete the exchange by replying in kind:

"I love you."

"Thank you. I love you, too."

We could also interpret saying, "I love you" as a way of showing vulnerability, of taking the risk of exposing our feelings to someone else to deepen our relationship. As with a gift, this interpretation also calls on the other person to reciprocate in some way. In either case, when we tell people that we love them—especially for the first time—we are hoping, if not expecting, that they will say they love us, too.

If the words have gone back and forth between us over a long period, we might assume the response even if it isn't actually spoken. But otherwise, if the reply falls short of "I love you, too," we have a problem. Such responses as "That's wonderful" or "Thank you for sharing that with me" or "It's great that you love me" are likely to leave us feeling dissatisfied, exposed, foolish, vulnerable, or even humiliated ("I told him that I love him, and all he said was 'Thank you'!"). Anyone who's gone out on the 'I love you' limb knows the special agony of waiting for the response. And anyone who's been on the receiving end without wanting to be knows how painfully awkward it is to feel obliged to reciprocate something you do not feel.

But couldn't we just fake a response to satisfy the obligation to reciprocate? People do this all the time in other situations:

"You look great today."

"Thanks, so do you."

We certainly could fake it, but we do so at our peril, because unlike saying, "You look great, too," 'I love you' is a powerful bit of performative language that amounts to far more than exchanging compliments and pleasant thoughts. In relationships that have a romantic potential (unlike, for example, the relationship between parents and children), saying, "I love you" for the first time is far more than a way to make someone feel good. It is also an invitation to alter a relationship. If we reciprocate with "I love you, too," we have done something that changes our relationship to the other person. Suddenly the expectations and understandings that connect us shift. There might, for example, be an expectation of adding a sexual dimension to the relationship or a preference for and loyalty toward that person above everyone else in all kinds of situations. We might even be expected to form a long-term if not permanent relationship that involves living together or forming a marriage and a family.

As performative language, the words do more than communicate, for they also act on social reality and transform it by altering our relationship with someone else. They are 'I do' on a less formally binding level and are important not simply for what they mean but for what they *do*. In this sense, all the positive feelings typically associated with saying, "I love you" are, without the performative words themselves, merely information without transformation:

"You say I'm wonderful, attractive, sexy, smart, and funny, that I excite you, interest you, and move you, and that you want to be with me. But you've never said you *love* me."

The words are crucial and powerful because they signal the crossing of a structural boundary around the love relationship. This is why we are so careful about when and to whom we say them. It is one thing to use just the word 'love,' as when signing a letter to a friend, for example, but quite another to say, "I love you." It is, in short, the difference between expressing a sentiment and declaring a relationship.

Using the words can take us across the boundary into a new relationship that radically alters our responsibilities and obligations. This difference between love as feeling and love as relationship is beautifully illustrated in the cult classic film *Harold and Maude*, in which a young and suicidally depressed Harold falls in love with the elderly, free-spirited Maude. Unbeknownst to Harold, Maude has a long-standing plan to end her life on her eightieth birthday, having decided that this will be the right time for her to die. She takes a drug overdose, and when Harold finds out, he rushes her to the hospital. Desperate to save her, he protests that she cannot do this because "I love you. I love you!" But she will not join him in his definition of feeling as a binding relationship: "Oh, Harold," she replies, "that's wonderful! Go and love some more!"

'I love you' works as performative language in many situations other than romantic ones, with quite different dynamics and results. When parents say, "I love you" to their children, for example, it means something different from when children say the same words to their parents. This reflects a profound difference in the roles of parent and child. For the parent, the words typically convey not only loving feelings but also a commitment to their children's well-being. The words are so closely tied to that commitment that they may not tell children much about how the parent actually feels toward them, which is why older children often make a distinction between being loved by parents and being liked. The role relationship between parents and children requires that parents love them in the sense of being committed to their care, but it does not require that parents like them.

From children's end of things, saying, "I love you" may not have much to do with how they actually feel toward parents, especially when they're too young to know much about what love is. Instead, the words can be a way to elicit reassurance from parents that the relationship is sure and certain, as shown when the parent reciprocates by saying, "I love you, too." This kind of ritual also works between adult partners as a shorthand way of signaling an ongoing commitment to the relationship.

The power of performative language requires us to use it with care. If we do not, we risk punishment reserved for people who show too little respect for its cultural authority and the harm its misuse can do. Nothing makes us unfit for social relationships as quickly as the habit of abusing performative language—the person who lies, breaks promises, betrays a trust, dodges responsibility for injury and loss, or professes love falsely or casually. In this sense, language is far more than talk, and we, in using it, are far more than mere talkers. We create and transform, spinning the world, ourselves, and one another as we speak.

Why Don't People Vote?

I'm writing this a few days before Election Day. As I think about what I plan to do this Tuesday, I am reminded that, if the past is any guide, tens of millions of eligible voters probably will not join me in exercising their constitutional right. Why they don't is a puzzle, especially given how many billions of people around the world have no right to vote in the first place, and even more of a puzzle when I consider that we are much less likely to vote than people in Canada, Japan, Australia, South Korea, and most of Europe.[2] What's going on?

If we look at the question sociologically, we have to begin with the principle that voting and not voting are two ways to participate in a political system. Given this idea, we have to ask how the political system is organized so that not voting appears as a path of least resistance for millions of people. Can a political system that celebrates democratic principles actually discourage people from voting?

Yes, it can, and it does.

To begin with, it is hard to register as a voter in the United States. Registration is automatic in Canada, for example, but in the United States you must apply in advance and be accepted as a voter. Recent laws make it possible to register as part of applying for a driver's license, but the right to vote still is not something that comes automatically with the fact of citizenship. Since a fairly high percentage of registered voters do vote, it is reasonable to assume that the easier it is to register, the more participation there will be.

That the United States is so reluctant to make registration easy reflects a long-standing cultural bias against the lower classes, newly arrived immigrants, and others who might use political power to disturb the status quo and the privilege of dominant groups. In the years following the revolution for independence that launched the great American 'experiment in democracy,' only white men who owned property were allowed to vote. The bias against voting continues today, as numerous states have enacted or proposed laws that would require people to show government-issued photo IDs to vote, a requirement that is especially difficult for the elderly and people living in poverty to meet.[3]

If we go deeper into the structure of the political system, we find that it is put together in ways that discourage people from registering or voting by taking away the potential for their vote to make a difference. Elections are organized on a winner-take-all principle, which means that to be represented in government, you must have a candidate who can win a majority of votes in a district. This requirement makes it impossible for minority points of view to be represented in state or federal legislatures unless the minority voters can put together a majority across an entire district, which is very hard to do. This situation appeared in a dramatic way in the decision to exclude third-party candidate Ross Perot from the 1996 presidential debates on the grounds that he didn't have a 'reasonable' chance of winning a majority of the national vote.

In contrast, most European parliaments apportion seats according to the percentage of the vote each party receives. If your party wins 5 percent of the vote, then your party gets 5 percent of the seats. But in the United States, a party could get as much as 49.99 percent of the vote without getting *any* seats. This means that if you support a candidate or party that cannot win a majority of all the votes in your district, it is easy to conclude that your vote won't make a difference. You might feel some moral satisfaction from doing your civic duty or protest by voting for 'none of the above' or for a candidate who shares your views but cannot possibly win. But your vote cannot result in your views being represented in the government. In a similar way, if your candidate is supported by a large majority, your additional vote has no effect on the overall level of representation for your views. European voters, however, can go to the polls knowing that each vote they cast will have a real additive effect that builds a political party's representation in the government.

Another reason that many people don't vote is that the U.S. political system has come to be organized around just two political parties. The Republicans and Democrats differ on some issues, such as abortion rights, same-sex marriage, and gun control, but they share an overall support for capitalism, wealth, property, and the use of military force to defend and advance national interests. They share a dependence on campaign contributions from corporations and other wealthy donors who expect politicians to serve their interests in return. They also share a reluctance to help people living in poverty who depend on welfare; a tendency to use immigrants, people in the lower class, teenage mothers, and people of color as scapegoats for social problems; and a resistance to doing anything serious about such problems as racism, sexism, and other forms of privilege and oppression.

If you belong to one of the groups whose interests the major parties do not support, then it's easy to see the political system as loaded toward interests that are not your own. From this perspective, it doesn't matter which party is in power. It also doesn't matter whether you vote, for the outcome for you will be the same either way. In 1996, for example, the federal government drastically cut welfare benefits and turned away from its long-standing commitment to care for its neediest citizens, including children living in poverty. The law was passed by a Republican-controlled Congress and signed by a Democratic president.

Since the 1990s, Republicans and Democrats have joined in what Harvard economist John Kenneth Galbraith describes as a "revolt of the contented against the unfortunate."[4] The United States has a political system controlled by a majority of the voting population, who are content with the way things are:

> It operates under the compelling cover of democracy, albeit a democracy not of all citizens but of those who, in defense of their social and economic advantage, actually go to the polls and vote. The result is a government accommodated not to reality or common need, but to the beliefs of the contented who are a majority of the actual voters.[5]

It should come as no surprise, then, that you are more likely to vote if you are in the middle or upper classes, have a good job, or are white.

An ecological factor in low voter turnout is a practice known as 'gerrymandering,' which is especially powerful in the election of congressional representatives. States are divided into congressional districts, and every ten years state legislatures redraw district lines based on population counts from the latest census. The goal of whichever party is in power is to draw district lines in such a way that voters favoring the opposing party are concentrated in as few districts as possible, minimizing the number of representatives they are able to elect. At the same time, lines are drawn so as to maximize the number of districts where substantial majorities of voters favor the incumbent party.[6]

One result of this practice is that voters find themselves in districts where the party they favor has such a large majority of supporters that their candidate is bound to win regardless of whether they vote. This means that each individual vote loses its importance, discouraging voters from bothering to show up at the polls since the outcome is perceived as all but certain.

It has become a common practice to explain low voter turnout in terms of psychological conditions, such as apathy. Sociologically, however, this misses the underlying fact that even if this were true for large numbers of potential voters, how people feel arises from their participation in social systems. When a political system is organized in ways that make staying away from the polls a rational choice for millions of people, it rings somewhat hollow to argue that citizens do not vote simply because they do not care, as if 'not caring' is a psychological condition that has no relation to the social systems in which people live their lives. It is striking to note that in the presidential campaign of 2008 that elected Barack Obama, voter turnout among people of color reached record levels, based on the perception that for the first time in generations, there was the possibility of electing a president who might actually make a positive difference in their lives, and their votes might play a role in making that happen.

Why Is There Poverty? Putting the 'Social' Back into Social Problems

Following the course of major social problems, such as poverty, drug abuse, violence, privilege, and oppression, it often seems that attempts to solve them never work. Government programs come and go as political parties swing back and forth between stock answers whose only effect seems to be influencing who gets elected. If anything, the problems get worse, and people feel increasingly helpless and frustrated or, if the problems do not affect them personally, may feel nothing much at all.

As a society, then, we are stuck, and we have been for a long time. One reason is that these social problems are huge and complex. But on a deeper level, we tend to think about them in ways that keep us from getting *at* their complexity in the first place. It is a basic tenet of sociological practice that to solve a social problem, we have to begin by seeing it as social,[7] without which we ask the wrong questions and look in the wrong direction for visions of change.

Consider poverty, for example, which is arguably the most far-reaching and long-standing cause of chronic suffering. The magnitude of poverty is especially ironic in the United States, whose enormous wealth dwarfs that of entire continents. Almost one out of every five people in the United States lives in poverty or near-poverty. For children, the rate is even higher.[8] Even people in the middle class have reason to feel anxious about the possibility of falling into poverty or something close to it—through divorce, for example, or being laid off as companies try to improve their competitive advantage, profit margins, and stock prices by replacing workers with machines or transferring jobs overseas.

How can there be so much misery and insecurity in the midst of such abundance? If we look at the question sociologically, one of the first things we notice is that poverty does not exist all by itself. It is one end of an overall distribution of income and wealth in society as a whole. As such, poverty is both a structural aspect of the system and an ongoing consequence of how the system is organized and the paths of least resistance that shape how people participate.

The economic system we have for producing and distributing wealth is industrial capitalism. It is organized in ways that allow a small elite to control most of the capital—factories, machinery, tools—used to produce wealth. This encourages the accumulation of wealth and income by the elite and regularly makes heroes of those who are most successful at it. It also leaves a relatively small portion of the total income and wealth to be divided among the rest of the population. With a majority of the people competing over what is left to them by the elite, it is inevitable that a substantial number of people will wind up on the short end and live in poverty or with the fear of it. It is like the game of musical chairs: since the game is set up with fewer chairs than there are people, someone *has* to wind up without a place to sit when the music stops.

In part, then, poverty exists because the economic system is organized in ways that encourage the accumulation of wealth at one end and create conditions of scarcity that make poverty inevitable at the other. But the capitalist system generates poverty in other ways as well.

In the drive for profit, for example, capitalism places a high value on competition and efficiency. This motivates companies and their managers to control costs by keeping wages as low as possible and replacing people with machines or replacing full-time workers with part-time workers. It makes it a path of least resistance to move jobs to regions or countries where labor is cheaper and workers are less likely to complain about poor working conditions or where laws protecting the natural environment from industrial pollution or workers from injuries on the job are weak or unenforced. Capitalism also encourages owners to shut down factories and invest money elsewhere in enterprises that offer higher rates of return.

These kinds of decisions are a normal consequence of how capitalism operates as a system, paths of least resistance that managers and investors are rewarded for following. But the decisions also have terrible effects on tens of millions of people and their families and, with them, entire communities. Even having a full-time job is no guarantee of a decent living, which is why so many families depend on the earnings of two or more adults just to make ends meet. This reality is made possible by the structural feature of capitalism by which most people neither own nor control any means of producing a living without working for someone else in exchange for wages.

To these social factors, we can add others. A high divorce rate, for example, results in large numbers of single-parent families who have a hard time depending on one adult for both child care and a living income. The centuries-old legacy of racism and white privilege in the United States continues to hobble millions of people through poor education, isolation in urban ghettos, prejudice, discrimination, and the disappearance of industrial jobs that, while requiring relatively little formal education, nonetheless once paid a decent wage. These were the jobs that enabled many generations of white European immigrants to climb out of poverty but which are now unavailable to the masses of urban poor.[9]

Clearly, patterns of widespread poverty are inevitable in an economic system that sets the terms for how wealth is produced and distributed. If we are interested in doing something about poverty itself—if we want a society largely free of impoverished citizens—then we have to do something about both the system people participate in and how they participate in it. But public debate about poverty and policies to deal with it focus almost entirely on how people participate, with almost nothing to say about the system they participate in. What generally pass for 'liberal' and 'conservative' approaches to poverty are, in fact, two variations on the same narrow theme of individualism.

A classic example of the conservative approach is Charles Murray's book *Losing Ground*.[10] Murray sees the world as a merry-go-round. The goal is to make sure that "everyone has a reasonably equal chance at the brass ring—or at least a reasonably equal chance to get on the merry-go-round."[11] He reviews thirty years of federal antipoverty programs and notes that they have generally failed. He concludes from this that since government programs have not worked, poverty must not be caused by social factors.

Instead, Murray argues, poverty is caused by failures of individual initiative and effort. People are poor because there is something lacking in them, and changing them is therefore the only effective remedy. From this he suggests doing away with public solutions, such as affirmative action, welfare, and income support systems, including "AFDC [aid to families with dependent children], Medicaid, food stamps, unemployment insurance, and the rest. Eliminating these programs would leave the working-aged person with no recourse whatsoever except the job market, family members, friends, and public or private locally funded services."[12] The result, he believes, would "make it possible to get as far as one can go on one's merit."[13] With the 1996 welfare reform act, the United States took a giant step in Murray's direction by reaffirming its long-standing cultural commitment to individualistic thinking and the mass of confusion around alternatives to it.

That confusion lies in how we think about individuals and society and about poverty as an individual condition and as a social problem. On the one hand, we can ask how individuals are sorted into different social class categories and which characteristics best predict who will get the best jobs and earn the most. If you want to get ahead, what's your best strategy? Based on many people's experience, the answer seems clear: work hard, get an education, and never give up.

There is certainly a lot of truth in this advice, and it gets to the issue of how people choose to participate in the system as it is. Sociologically, however, it focuses on only one part of the equation by leaving out the system itself. In other words, it ignores the fact that social life is shaped by the nature of systems *and* how people participate, by the forest *and* the trees. Changing how individuals participate may affect outcomes for some. As odd as this may seem, however, it has relatively little to do with the larger question of why widespread poverty exists at all as a social phenomenon.

Imagine for a moment that income is distributed according to the results of a footrace: all the income in the United States for each year is put into a giant pool, and we hold a race to determine who gets what. The fastest fifth of the population gets 50 percent of the income to divide up, the next fastest fifth splits 23 percent, the next fastest fifth gets 15 percent, the next fifth 9 percent, and the slowest fifth divides 3 percent. The result would be an unequal distribution of income, with each person in the fastest fifth getting 16.7 times as much money as each person in the slowest fifth, which is what the actual distribution of income in the United States looks like.[14]

If we look at the slowest fifth of the population and ask why they are poor, an obvious answer is that they didn't run as fast as everyone else, and if they could just run faster, they would do better. This prompts us to ask why some people run faster than others and to consider all kinds of answers from genetics to nutrition to motivation to having time to work out to being able to afford a personal trainer.

But to see why *some* fifth of the population *must* be poor no matter how fast people run, all we have to do is look at the system itself. It uses unbridled competition to determine not only who gets fancy cars and nice houses but also who gets to eat or has a place to live or access to health care. It distributes income and wealth in ways that promote increasing concentrations among those who already have the most. Given this, some of the people in this year's bottom fifth might run faster next year and leave others to take their place in the bottom fifth. But there *has* to be a bottom fifth, so long as the system is organized in this way.

Some argue that a different solution is to increase the amount of income available, to create a 'bigger pie' as a way to raise people out of poverty. As the history of capitalism makes painfully clear, however, the same system that enables the upper classes to take most of the national income every year also enables them to absorb any increases in the income pool. Between 2009 and 2012, for example, as the economy was recovering from the disaster of 2008, the top 1 percent of the population received *95 percent* of the total growth in national income.[15]

Learning to run faster may keep you or me out of poverty, but it will not get rid of poverty itself. To do that, we have to change the system along with how people participate in it. Using the footrace metaphor, instead of splitting the 'winnings' into shares of 50 percent, 23 percent, 15 percent, 9 percent, and 3 percent, for example, we might divide them into shares of 24 percent, 22 percent, 20 percent, 18 percent, and 16 percent. There would still be inequality, but the fastest fifth would get only 1.5 times as much as the bottom instead of 16.7 times as much, and 1.2 times as much as the middle fifth rather than 3.3 times as much.

People can argue about whether chronic widespread poverty is morally acceptable or what an acceptable level of inequality might look like. But if we want to understand where poverty comes from and what makes it such a stubborn feature of social life, we have to begin with the sociological fact that patterns of inequality result as much from how social systems are organized as they do from how individuals participate. Focusing on one without the other simply will not produce a solution.

The focus on individuals is so entrenched in our culture, however, that even those who believe they are taking social factors into account usually are not. This is as true of Murray's critics as it is of Murray himself. Perhaps Murray's greatest single mistake is to misinterpret the failure of federal antipoverty programs. He assumes that federal programs actually target the social causes of poverty, which means that if the programs do not work, social causes must not be the issue.

But Murray has it wrong. Welfare and other antipoverty programs are 'social' only in the sense of being organized around the idea that social systems, such as government, have a responsibility to do something about poverty. But the antipoverty programs themselves are *not* organized around a sociological understanding of how systems *produce* poverty in the first place. As a result, they focus almost entirely on changing individuals and not systems and use the resources of government and other systems to make it happen.

If antipoverty programs have failed, it is not because the idea that poverty is socially caused is wrong. They have failed because policy makers who design them do not understand what makes the cause of something 'social' in the first place. Or they understand it but are so trapped in individualistic thinking that they do not act on it by targeting the appropriate systems, such as the economy, for serious change.

The easiest way to see this is to look at the antipoverty programs themselves, which come in two main varieties. The first holds individuals responsible by assuming that financial success is solely a matter of individual qualifications and behavior. In other words, if you just run faster, you'll finish the race ahead of people who are currently beating you, and then *they* will be poor instead of you. We get people to run faster by providing training and motivation. What we do not do, however, is look at the rules of the race or question whether the basic necessities of life should be distributed through competition.

The result is that some people rise out of poverty by improving their competitive advantage, while others sink into it when their advantages no longer work and they get laid off or their company relocates to another country or gets swallowed up in a merger that boosts the stock price for shareholders and earns the CEO a salary that in 2012 averaged more than 273 times the average worker's pay.[16] But rarely is anything said—much less done—about an economic system that allows a small elite to own and control most of the wealth and that sets up the rest of the population to compete over what is left.

This is why the Occupy Wall Street movement created such a stir when it burst on the scene in 2011 with its critique of not only capitalism but also the power and influence of corporations and the wealthy over federal and state governments. In spite of its beginning, it has failed thus far to grow into a larger movement, in part because it has not been guided by a comprehensive sociological analysis of the problem.

In the meantime, individuals rise and fall in the class system, and the stories of those who rise are offered as proof of what is possible, while the stories of those who fall are offered as cautionary tales. The system itself—including the huge gap between the wealthy and everyone else and the steady proportion of people living in poverty—stays the same.

A second type of antipoverty program seems to assume that individuals are not to blame for their impoverished circumstances, because it reaches out with various kinds of aid that help people meet day-to-day needs. Welfare payments, food stamps, housing subsidies, and Medicaid soften the impact of poverty, for example, but they do little about the steady supply of people living in poverty. There is nothing wrong with this approach in that it can lessen the amount of suffering. But it should not be seen as a way to solve poverty, no more than army field hospitals can stop wars.

In relation to poverty as a social problem, welfare and other such programs are like doctors who keep giving bleeding patients transfusions without repairing the wounds. In effect, Murray tells us that federal programs just throw good blood after bad. In a sense, he is right, but not for the reasons he gives. Murray would merely substitute one ineffective individualistic solution for another. If we do as he suggests and throw people on their own, certainly some will find a way to run faster than they did before. But that will not do anything about the 'race' or the overall patterns of inequality that result from using it as a way to organize one of the most important aspects of human life.[17]

Liberals and conservatives are locked in a tug of war between two individualistic solutions to problems that are only partly about individuals. Both approaches rest on profound misunderstandings of what makes a problem, such as poverty, social. Neither is informed by a sense of how social life actually works as a dynamic relation between social systems and how people participate. This misunderstanding is also what traps them between blaming such problems as poverty on individuals and blaming them on society. Solving social problems does not require us to choose or blame one or the other. It does require us to see how the two combine to shape the terms of social life and how people actually live it.

Because social problems are more than an accumulation of individual woes, *they cannot be solved through an accumulation of individual solutions.* We must include social solutions that take into account how economic, political, and other systems really work. We also have to identify the paths of least resistance that produce the same patterns and problems year after year. This means that capitalism can no longer occupy its near-sacred status that holds it immune from criticism. It may mean that capitalism is in some ways incompatible with a just society in which the excessive well-being of some does not require the misery of so many others. It will not be easy to face up to such possibilities, but if we don't, we will guarantee poverty its future and all the conflict and suffering that go with it.

Making Men's Violence Invisible

As we saw in the Chapter 1 discussion of suicide, when behavior and experience vary by such characteristics as gender, age, and race, it raises questions about the relationship between people and the systems in which they participate. Whether we are comparing women to men or Japanese to Hungarians, the focus is on the kind of observable patterns that tip us off that something social is going on.

The word 'observable' brings up a pattern that is itself important, which is that some patterns are more likely to be noticed than others. For example, considerable public attention is paid to how patterns of teenage girls getting pregnant vary by race, education, and social class. But there is little mention of the equally—if not more—important pattern of young adult men impregnating teenage girls. Since impregnation is an essential cause of pregnancy, you would think this pattern would be of great interest, but it's not. The behavior of teenage girls is scrutinized, but not the behavior of men.

The invisibility of men's problematic behavior is even more true of the global epidemic of violence, ranging from battery, rape, suicide, and murder to mass murder, terrorism, and war. Since the overwhelming majority of violence is perpetrated by men, one would expect a great deal of interest in how a single social status could account for so much violence, but the reality is just the opposite—the phrase 'men's violence' rarely appears in public conversation, even when that is the focus of attention.

In 2012, for example, two major mass murders occurred in the United States, one in a movie theater in Aurora, Colorado, and the other in an elementary school in Newtown, Connecticut. In the news coverage that followed, experts were asked why such things happen and, in particular, what the shooters had in common that might explain their behavior. In each case, the answer was the same: the murderers had different *psychological* profiles and therefore did not conform to any pattern that might help provide an explanation. In one news report, photographs of these and several other shooters were arranged in a row—all white males—and still the experts said they had nothing in common. Even when the news anchor pointed out that all were white males, the response was to ignore the question. This observable pattern of 'not seeing' the gender pattern is repeated routinely from politicians to newspaper op-ed pages.

This, then, is the sociological puzzle: why is there so much silence about men's violence? Why has it become 'normal' to act as if this clear and unambiguous pattern isn't there?

On the most basic level, the silence comes from using an individualistic model of the world that interprets 'men's violence' on the basis of the assumption that nothing exists beyond the individual. To ask, then, what it means that most violence is perpetrated by men appears to link violence not simply with the individual men who do it but with the simple fact of *being* a man. Since the word 'men' is taken to mean all individual men grouped together, any question about 'men's violence' is bound to be seen as an accusation that all men are violent. Many will then object that most men are not violent, which, of course, is true, but this response can stop the conversation right there or, more often, keep it from starting in the first place. Hence the silence.

If our point of view is sociological, however, the meaning of 'men's violence' is quite different. 'Men' now refers to something more than a sum of individual men. It takes on a larger meaning by naming a social category in a social system, a position that locates people in relation to a social context that shapes their experience and behavior. Now questions about 'men's violence' also have a larger meaning: Is it significant that the overwhelming majority of perpetrators of violence occupy the same social status? Is there something about the paths of least resistance that go along with that position that might explain the pattern? These are the questions about 'men's violence' that really need to be asked, but we never get that far because the individualistic model takes us down a path that leads to a dead end of defensive arguments about whether all men are violent or nonviolent, good or bad.   *for lace also*

Whether a category of people is made visible or invisible depends on its position in a social system. In systems of privilege, things done by members of subordinate groups that make their group look bad are likely to be noticed and portrayed as characteristic of the group as whole, because this supports the idea that they are inferior and deserve to be subordinate. In contrast, things that make them look good tend to be overlooked or seen as a reflection of only the exceptional individual (the presidential election of Barack Obama, for example, and his popularity among voters were accompanied by an *increase* rather than a decrease in prejudicial views of black people in general among white people).[18] For dominant groups, the pattern is reversed: men's violence is seen only in relation to individual men who commit violent acts. It is not seen as something arising from a system of male privilege in which violence is a path of least resistance for men to follow themselves or to support in other men. The result is that violent men are perceived as having nothing in common with one another or the male population as a whole.

This double standard is enforced in part by the fact that dominant groups have a great deal of power. By controlling virtually every major social institution, from the economy and government to higher education and the mass media, men also control jobs, resources, and the flow of information, including what kinds of questions are pursued and reported by journalists, discussed by politicians, and researched by social scientists.

The protective cloak of silence surrounding men's violence goes still deeper into the structural and cultural underpinnings of the system of male privilege. Women and men, for example, experience intimate and dependent relationships with each other, especially in families. This would be impossible without our being able to believe that, unless they show otherwise, the men in our lives—fathers, sons, brothers, husbands, friends, lovers—are 'good' men with whom we are safe. Because gender is part of what defines so many important relationships, and because intimacy requires a level of trust that makes us vulnerable to others, we have a deep interest in believing that violence is *not* gendered, that gender is *not* a determining factor in either the cause of violence or in who winds up as perpetrators or victims.

It is no small thing, then, to identify 'men's violence' as something that is not only a real phenomenon but also the basis for an ongoing and often terrifying epidemic reported in the daily news. If this particular man, this mother's son, this woman's husband, this child's father, whom everyone thought was kind and decent, can do such things, then what is it that makes us believe some other man, someone we know, will not?

An even larger and deeper level lies beneath the silence, one that goes beyond concerns about the individual men in our lives. In a patriarchal worldview,* manhood is defined as not only an ideal for men and boys but also a universal standard that applies to everyone, the purest expression of what it means to be a superior human being. Patriarchal manhood is a prerequisite to greatness, the defining attribute for any position that is culturally defined as worthy of honor, admiration, and respect. Any woman who aspires to be president, for example, or a firefighter, a soldier, a corporate CEO, or a hero of any kind will be measured by the standard of patriarchal manhood, while a man will not be judged on his ability to meet the expectations of womanhood.[19]

The patriarchal ideal of manhood also applies to our society itself, to the idea of America and what it means to be American. Every society has a cultural mythology, the living collection of images and stories, folktales and songs, documents and history lessons, films and anthems, monuments, flags, speeches, and commemorations that we rely on to tell us who we are and what our nation is about. Richard Slotkin's account of the origins and evolution of the American mythology reveals a national story that for hundreds of years has centered on men and their ability to dominate and control.[20] The objects of that control have included the Earth and its nonhuman species, Native Americans, Mexicans, and others who refused to surrender their land to American expansion, enslaved Africans and other peoples of color whose exploited labor was indispensable to American wealth and power, Southern secession and rebellion, white workers and immigrants, Filipinos who refused to let their country become a colony of the United States following the Spanish-American War, and a long list of nations and groups considered to be a threat to American interests.[21]

From *The Last of the Mohicans* and 'Custer's Last Stand' to 'The Greatest Generation' of World War II and the U.S. Navy SEALs storming the refuge

---

*A 'worldview' is the collection of interconnected beliefs, values, attitudes, images, stories, and memories out of which a sense of reality is constructed and maintained in a social system and the minds of individuals who participate in it. It includes everything from the assumption that gravity will hold us down to a belief in God.

of Osama bin Laden, the focus of the American story has been not merely on men but on a masculine view of national strength, pride, superiority, and exceptionalism, the liberty and power to dominate the world and act without restraint. All of this is ultimately backed by a capacity for violence and the willingness to use it.

Theodore Roosevelt, for example, who was twice elected to the presidency, stated repeatedly that the most important measure of America's national strength is its *virility*, that to be truly American is to *be* virile, and that virility has no higher or more powerful expression than a nation's ability to impose its will on others, including, and especially, through the use of violence.[22] Presidents since Roosevelt may have been less explicit, the language more encoded, but the mythology has remained the same: nothing matches the kind of national angst and outrage that follow an American combat defeat or the thrill that comes with victory. And there are few ways to more quickly cast doubt on presidential leadership than for the commander in chief to show a reluctance to use force.

The people of the United States have not, of course, been of one mind about this story. There has always been vocal and sometimes passionate dissent. But violent manhood as an instrument of American will and an indicator of national character and greatness has ruled the day almost from the beginning. With the exception of the Vietnam War, the withholding or withdrawal of public support has not been prompted by the belief that the use of violence was wrong or excessive, but because a war has not been *successful*, a failure to win in a timely way. With recent wars in Iraq and Afghanistan, public support weakened only because the wars came to be seen as going on for too long and not worth the monetary cost and continued loss of American lives.[23] There has, however, been no national outpouring of opposition or regret, much less shame, for the suffering and loss of life in local populations resulting from the U.S. invasion of these countries.

Manhood and the capacity for violence are not, of course, the whole of the American cultural mythology, but without them and the consequences they have and continue to produce, the story would be all but unrecognizable. This is why so much is at stake in the decision of whether to openly acknowledge the reality of men's violence, for to do that is to risk confronting the principle of dominance and control that lies at the core of the patriarchal worldview that, in turn, informs and shapes individual lives and our society as a whole. To avoid that, we focus on what we tell ourselves is nothing more than the actions of a few evil or crazy individuals rather than question the patriarchal system and its core principles that underlie American manhood and its connection to violence.

From love to poverty, from voting to violence, the reality of social life comes in layers and dimensions that often go unnoticed and unexamined. The power of sociological practice lies in its unique worldview, from which we can connect those layers and dimensions to provide a coherent understanding of social systems and how we live our lives in relation to them.

7

Sociology as Worldview

Where White Privilege Came From

Like most students, when I was first studying sociology, I thought I was acquiring a body of knowledge—facts and concepts and how to use various intellectual and practical tools for creating new knowledge through research and thinking creatively about the human condition. What I did not realize until much later was that I was also changing my worldview, the largely unconscious collection of beliefs and values out of which we construct what we take to be reality itself.

The idea, for example, that we are always participating in something larger than ourselves—social systems that we can observe, describe, and understand—is not one that I grew up with or that I see in use even now when I observe the world. Most people, from the president of the United States to my casual friends, seem to live inside an individualistic worldview that, in this way, is quite different than the one described in these pages. As a result, when we observe the world, we tend to ask very different questions because, literally, we are experiencing the reality of things in ways that are themselves quite different.

A news item about poverty in America, for example, reports that the percentage of people living in poverty not only is high but also has remained unchanged for more than six years in spite of the so-called recovery from the economic collapse of 2008. The individualistic worldview prompts the reporter to ask how we can improve the lives of people living in poverty by changing their individual circumstances (such as welfare benefits, Medicaid, food stamps, and unemployment insurance) or the kind of people they are (such as education, job training, and attitude adjustments). In contrast, I *also* want to know how social systems can be changed so that as all kinds of people participate, poverty will be far less likely to result in the country as a whole. Different realities, different questions, and different answers make all the difference.

The sociological worldview I've described in this book is not, in its most basic ideas and principles, a very complicated thing, which is one of my favorite things about it, because it also has such power to shape how we perceive and interpret reality and the kinds of questions we ask about what we do not know. But it is also powerful, I believe, because it *works*, because it is grounded in the reality of how things are in a way that individualistic thinking is not.

One of the most important things I've learned from sociological practice is that the relationship between systems and the people who participate in them is profoundly *dynamic.* The patterns of social life that result from people going about their lives by following paths of least resistance are predictable, and yet we can never know for sure what we are going to do from one moment to the next. The result is that nothing really stays the same, no matter how much it may seem to. Systems are always being created and re-created—their cultures, their structural patterns, their ecological arrangements, their population dynamics. And, in important ways, *we* are always being created and re-created as social beings interacting with people as participants in one system or another.

A sociological worldview is also powerful because it works on every level, from a simple conversation to global politics. The bottom half of Figure 4 shows the relationship between systems and people that we first looked at in Chapter 1. But now we are in a position to say more about the nature of social systems and how social life actually happens. Every system has various characteristics, as shown in the top half of the model, and these are all connected to one another. This is to say, for example, that changes in structure may prompt changes in culture or in the dynamics of population and human ecology, just as changes in culture can lead to changes in the other two.

The only reason it is important to understand social life is that it produces consequences that matter, which is what drew me to sociology in the first place. Those consequences include everything that happens as we par-

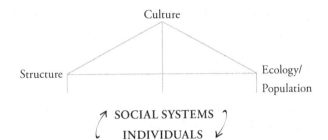

Figure 4. A model for sociological thinking.

ticipate in social systems—*every*thing, no matter how small and inconsequential or how large and profound, from two people accidentally bumping into each other while getting on a bus ("Excuse me." "No problem.") to the legal definition of marriage, conflict between social classes, global warming, war, and the fate of the Earth. Some consequences are external to social systems, such as the extinction of various species of life as a result of global warming (although the *cause* of that warming itself has everything to do with social systems). The rest, however, take place in the context of social systems, including the characteristics of systems themselves, such as cultural beliefs or norms or the distribution of power. The result is an unending cycle of movement and change through which social life happens on multiple levels and people's lives happen in relation to it.

Part of what changes are worldviews themselves, including sociology, which came into being as a product of social life only a few centuries ago and has been changing ever since. Like everything else, worldviews are both a consequence of social life and what makes everything else possible by shaping our sense of reality. The idea of race, for example, as a core element of the American worldview with profound consequences over hundreds of years *came* from somewhere as a result of people participating in certain social systems during a particular period of history—which puts us in the interesting position of using one worldview to understand another.

Where White Privilege Came From

The history of white privilege is a long and complicated story, too long and too complicated for me to tell completely here,[1] but what I can do is identify major aspects of the story as a way to show how the sociological model works.

We begin with the long history of the British struggle to conquer Ireland and subjugate its people. This structural relation of domination along with British frustration in the face of stubborn resistance gave rise to a cultural belief that the Irish were an inferior and savage people, not merely in the organization of their societies but in their nature as human beings. The British came to see the Irish as something like a separate species altogether, possessing inferior traits that were biologically passed from one generation to the next.

In perceiving the Irish in this way, the British were changing their worldview by creating a concept of race that encouraged them to see other peoples as subhuman if not inhuman. By not seeing them as members of their own kind, they saw them instead as objects to be controlled through any means necessary, not as human beings whose suffering might be an occasion for empathy and restraint. Using such a worldview, it would seem to the British both reasonable and right that they would assert control through the use of force, much as they would over the land or nonhuman animals.

When the British came to North America in the seventeenth century, they brought with them a worldview that included the idea of race and a view of themselves as a people destined to dominate any land in which they might choose to establish themselves. To this was added the explosive growth of industrial capitalism as an economic system in the eighteenth and nineteenth centuries, whose structure is organized around capitalists' ability to control the conditions and resources on which profit depends.

In the early stages of capitalism, for example, markets were the object of control, as capitalists bought goods in one place and took them to another where they were in scarce supply and could command a higher price than the one they originally paid. Later, as capitalists became involved in the production of goods, profit depended more on the ability to control workers and natural resources than on markets—the less the capitalist pays for labor and materials, the more is left over for the capitalist to keep.

The ecology of North America lent itself to agriculture on a massive scale, and the capitalist demand for land and cheap labor far outstripped the available supply. Most of the land that was to become the United States was gained through a system of military and political dominance over Native Americans, a campaign of deceit, broken treaties, and military conquest that included the use of forced migration (now known as ethnic cleansing) and genocide, practices that today would be considered crimes against humanity.[2]

Most of the labor was drawn from the population of indentured European servants, Native Americans, and Africans, none of whom was initially held in a state of perpetual slavery. The structure of the capitalist system, however, and the British worldview in which they saw themselves as an inherently and distinctly superior race of people combined to lay down a path of least resistance leading in that direction.

Attempts to convert indentured white servants to permanent slaves failed because most were from England and had too strong a sense of their rights as individuals to allow it. It proved equally impractical to enslave Native Americans, because they could easily escape and disappear among native populations. This left black Africans, who were not among their own people in their own land and whose physical features made them stand out among the rest of the population, leaving them with no place to hide should they manage to run away. They alone were selected for the status of permanent slavery.

Complicating the process, however, was the existence of sacred cultural beliefs and values on which the fledgling democracy was founded. The Declaration of Independence and the Constitution with its Bill of Rights clearly contradict such practices as genocide, conquest, forced migration, slavery, the buying and selling of human beings, and the denial of basic rights to dignity, self-determination, and freedom.

To resolve the contradiction, the concept of race was invoked to create cultural categories of 'white' and 'nonwhite' human beings. Native Americans, whose societies Thomas Jefferson had regarded as equal to those of Europeans—and in some ways superior—were increasingly regarded as biologically and socially inferior and doomed either to be absorbed into the English way of life or made to disappear altogether.

Unlike Native Americans, however, Africans were held in a state of perpetual bondage that extended to their biological descendants. Because of this, the concept of race was carried to an extreme by defining white people as a separate and biologically superior species and black people as innately inferior and therefore incapable of learning or advancing themselves. This view, in turn, was used to justify holding black people in a permanent status of subordination to white people, on whom they supposedly were to depend for guidance and discipline. It was a common belief among white people that they were doing Africans a favor by bringing them to live in service as a kind of deliverance from what they assumed was an inferior and savage existence in Africa.

It is important to emphasize that prior to the British experience with the Irish and the enslavement of Africans in North America, the cultural concept of race, including such categories as 'white' and 'color' as social markers of inferiority and superiority, did not exist.[3] Notice, then, how cultural ideas can come into being as a way to justify structural arrangements and how those same ideas can go on to play a role in shaping other systems in various ways, such as the subordination of Africans and Native Americans when English migrants came to North America to make new lives for themselves. This kind of interaction among the various characteristics of social systems is basic to understanding how social life happens—everything is connected to and has the potential to affect everything else.

Structural patterns of dominance also operate among whites, of course, and the concept of race has played a role in this as well. In the nineteenth century, for example, white people in dominant classes carried out a campaign to encourage lower- and working-class white people to think of themselves as white—to make the ascribed status of 'white' an important part of their social identity and worldview. This was offered as a form of compensation for their miserable situation as workers, as in 'I may be poor, but at least I'm white.'[4]

Since then, racial identity has played an important role in distracting white workers from the realities of capitalism by encouraging them to focus on race instead of class. At the turn of the twentieth century, for example, when the labor movement was at its peak, unions routinely excluded workers of color. When white unions went on strike to enforce demands for better working conditions, employers often brought in people of color as strikebreakers, hoping white workers would channel their energy and anger into issues of race and away from the reasons that caused them to go on strike in the first place. Today, similar dynamics operate around issues related to affirmative action and immigration policy.

This history happened through the participation of individual people in social systems of various kinds, but it is important to note that none of it *had* to happen as it did. The characteristics of systems produce paths of least resistance for people to follow, but nothing in the nature of those paths precludes the possibility of people choosing otherwise.

There was, for example, overwhelming support for the doctrine of Manifest Destiny as part of the American worldview that was used to justify the conquest of new territory and the practice of slavery, but there was also opposition. The abolitionist movement, for example, was based on a radically different worldview when it came to the subject of race and slavery. And protesters like Henry David Thoreau were willing to go to prison rather than pay taxes to fund a war against Mexico instigated solely to enlarge the United States by taking Mexican land. People who participate in social systems, in short, are not robots or puppets in relation to them and their dominant worldview. A system's characteristics can load the odds in ways that create paths of least resistance, but the rest depends on what people choose to do from one moment to the next.

Most of the choices we make are unconscious, it being in the nature of paths of least resistance to make our choices appear to be the logical, normal things to do without our having to think about them. This means, of course, that we can participate in systems in ways we are not aware of, help produce consequences without knowing it, and be involved in other people's lives, historically and in the present, without any intention to do so. I came to this awareness for myself through tracing my own family's connection to the history of the United States, including white privilege and racism.

On the face of it, the path of least resistance is for me to jump to the conclusion that since, as far as I know, I do not behave in overtly racist ways and since my ancestors are not from the South and did not own slaves, this troubling history has nothing to do with me. But the history of race in this country and how it plays out today show that things are more complicated than that.

My mother's grandfather, for example, migrated from Connecticut to Wisconsin, where he bought land and started what became a prosperous dairy farm. As it turns out, the land he purchased had been taken from the Ho-Chunk Native American tribe several decades earlier, even though the federal government had promised to protect forever their rights to their ancestral homeland. That promise was honored only until white miners showed an interest in rich deposits of lead on Ho-Chunk land, and so the United States reneged on its promise and called in its army to force the Ho-Chunk from their land in spite of the treaty.

From the Ho-Chunk point of view, my great-grandfather had purchased stolen property, but since white people had the power to make and enforce the law, they could also decide what was stolen and what was not, and so he was allowed to purchase the land without a second thought. He went on to be a successful farmer in the midst of the booming U.S. economy that, as the saying goes, was a rising tide that lifted all boats, including his. For people of color, however, who were systematically denied the opportunity to own their own 'boats,' the rising industrial capitalist tide brought little benefit.

When my great-grandfather died, the farm was inherited by my grandfather, and when my grandparents died, it was sold, and my mother and her four siblings each received a share of the proceeds. And when my parents bought their first house in 1954, they used her modest inheritance for the down payment. They also obtained an affordable mortgage from the Federal Housing Administration (FHA), which was set up after World War II to help returning veterans buy their own homes. Being ordinary citizens, they may well have been unaware of the fact that federal regulations and guidelines governing FHA loans overwhelmingly favored whites over veterans of color, putting them on the receiving end of white privilege in one of the biggest transfers of wealth in U.S. history. Regardless of whether my parents knew it, however, the effect was the same.[5]

My parents now had a 'boat' of their own that was lifted by the rising tide of an expanding economy in the 1950s and 1960s, and when my wife and I wanted to buy our first house in the 1980s and didn't have enough money for the down payment, we borrowed it from my mother. Now we had a boat that we were able to sell some years later so that we could then build the house that we are living in now—a house that, I recently learned, is sitting on land that was once part of the homeland of the Massacoe tribe, from whom it was taken by white people in the seventeenth century. The method by which it was taken was illegal under colonial law, but when those who took the land offered to share it with the colony, the officials decided not to interfere.

I could say this history has nothing personally to do with me, that it was all a long time ago and caused by someone else, that my ancestors were all good, moral, and decent people who never killed or enslaved anyone or drove anyone from their land. Even if that were true (I'll never know for sure), the only way to let it go at that is to ignore the fact that if someone were willing to take the time to follow the money, they would find that some portion of the house and land that we now call home can be traced directly back through my family history to the laws and practices that white people have collectively imposed through their government and other institutions, back to the capitalist Industrial Revolution and the exploitation of people of color that made it possible, and back to the conquest, forced expulsion, and genocide through which the land that is now the United States was first acquired by Europeans. In other words, some portion of this house is our share of the benefits of white privilege passed on and accumulated from one generation to the next.

For some white people, the share of benefits is greater or less than for others, depending on, among other things, the dynamics of social class. But one thing is certain: collectively, the white population of the United States now holds an enormous unearned advantage of wealth and power. Regardless of what kind of people we are as individuals or what we have or have not done ourselves, that advantage cannot be uncoupled from the history of race and racism in this country. The past is more than history. It is also present in structural distributions of wealth and power and cultural ideologies, laws, practices, beliefs, and attitudes whose effect is to justify, defend, and perpetuate the system of white privilege. And the past is present in the huge moral dilemmas that arise from such a history and the question of what to do about the unnecessary suffering and injustice that continue to result from it.

The path of least resistance in any system is to adhere to a worldview in which none of these considerations are acknowledged and to accept the organization of social life as just the way things are and were always meant to be. This is especially true of dominant groups in systems of privilege, who can indulge in the luxury of obliviousness, the freedom to live unaware of the system they participate in and how and with what effect.

By contrast, there is no moment of greater awareness for anyone than when they step off the path of least resistance and both the path and the system of which it is a part become visible. There is also no moment of greater potential to make a difference. In 1960, for example, most public accommodations were racially segregated throughout the American South. One day, in Greensboro, North Carolina, four young African American college students walked into a Woolworth's and bought school supplies for their first term in college and then sat down at the lunch counter and asked for menus. The waitress, however, refused to serve them—"We don't serve your kind here"—and told them to leave.[6]

They were furious at being treated this way, being from Northern cities where racism and segregation were certainly alive and well but not in such a blatant form. For weeks, they argued among themselves about what to do, until finally they decided to return to the lunch counter and refuse to leave until they were served like everyone else. As they sat on the stools that day, they were threatened, verbally abused, and physically manhandled and had food and drink thrown on them, and yet they refused to leave. Finally, the manager announced that the lunch counter was closed. As the students rose to leave, they said they would return the next day. And they did, along with others who had heard of their actions, and then still more the day after that, until every seat was occupied by a person of color openly defying the overt racial segregation that had been a hallmark of the South for hundreds of years.

Within a matter of weeks, news of what happened in Greensboro spread and prompted similar sit-ins across North Carolina and then, within a few months, throughout the South in all kinds of public accommodations. The eventual result was an end to this form of segregation.

Notice what these young men did and did not do. They did not try to change anyone's mind. They did not speak, much less argue, with anyone or hand out written statements. Instead, they made use of the fact that every social system happens only through the participation of individuals, any one of whom has the potential to change how the system happens by stepping off the path of least resistance. By changing the way the system happened, they changed that thing larger than themselves that shapes people's experience, behavior, and expectations about what is *supposed* to happen from one moment to the next. In other words, they discovered that changing the way a system happens is a far more powerful—and potentially more dangerous—strategy than trying to change individuals one at a time.

Notice also how their choices fit into the sociological model. By stepping off the path of least resistance, they changed the ecology and the structure of that small system known as a lunch counter. They altered patterns of interaction and the arrangement of people in physical space, which is the essence of segregation. Their actions challenged not only the distribution of power that had kept these arrangements in place as cornerstones of white privilege but also the worldview of race that had made it seem the natural order of things. This, in turn, produced all kinds of consequences, including tension and conflict and the manager closing the lunch counter and more people showing up the next day and so on, all of which continued to affect how the system happened from one moment to the next. Those consequences reverberated from that small place to much larger systems, and on and on from there, including my retelling of the story in these pages and whatever effect this might have on the people who read it and the people whose lives they will affect.

This is how social life happens and how it may change. But notice that for all the years of struggle over civil rights, white privilege is still alive and well in the United States. Why? In part, it is because white elites have the power to slow the pace of change by controlling social institutions. But a deeper answer lies in the dominant worldview that makes the reality of race either appear as normal and acceptable or not appear at all, to be invisible. To understand change, then, and how it is resisted, we must also understand something more about worldviews that makes us reluctant to give them up.

A Worldview Is Hard to Change

The history of white privilege depended on the cultural invention of the ideas of race in general and whiteness in particular as part of a radical shift in the European worldview. It helped create a taken-for-granted reality in which an institution like slavery might appear not only to 'make sense' but also to be morally acceptable, if not an act of virtue in the fulfillment of God's intention.

So, too, does our understanding of that history depend on a sociological worldview that is itself at odds with the prevailing worldview in our society. In part, this conflict is due to the tendency of many sociologists to focus on issues of social justice and inequality, a perspective that has always been a minority point of view. But the main reason for the sociological worldview's not taking hold in the United States is that it directly conflicts with the individualistic model that is the bedrock of our culture.

If we were to adopt the view that social life happens through a dynamic relation between people and social systems, it would upend the American fixation on the individual, a core part of our worldview that endures in spite of the fact that it is not based in reality. This would also challenge the use of individualism as a way to rationalize inequality and oppression so as to protect privilege in all its forms. It is no surprise, then, that sociology is often viewed as a somewhat alien way of thinking: in the context of the dominant American worldview, it is.

Worldviews are resistant to change because we depend on them as the sum total of what we know or think we know or just assume, consciously or not, a vast collection of interconnected beliefs, values, attitudes, images, and memories. Most of the time a worldview provides the deep unconscious background that enables us to navigate reality from one moment to the next. It shapes how we see everything, from the cosmos and what happens when we die to why people do what they do. It provides the material out of which we construct a taken-for-granted reality that we do not have to question or even think about. It shapes not only what we perceive as real but also how we make sense of it, how we explain what happens and what is and is not, and how we justify what we do in any given situation. Even more powerful is that we tend not to be aware that worldviews even exist or of how complex they are. Expose one part to scrutiny and doubt and you cannot help but bring others into question.

When I consider why it is so hard to change a worldview—whether someone else's or my own—I find that it depends on how it came to be there, what authority is behind it, and how 'centrally located' or interconnected it is in relation to the rest. My worldview, for example, includes the belief that the Earth is roughly 4.5 billion years old. That bit of reality was added when I read about it somewhere. I do not remember where or when it was, but I do know I adopted this piece of information because the source was identified as science, and my worldview includes a general trust in what scientists claim as true, knowing all the while that it can change as new evidence comes to light. Adding this belief to my worldview happened in a particular moment in a particular way and from a particular source, and I could have decided against it or withheld judgment for one reason or another, as I sometimes do.

What I take to be real about the age of the Earth is a simple and isolated piece of my and many other people's worldview. It is not connected to other beliefs that matter to me and has little effect on my life, so I don't really care whether it's true and would not hesitate to give it up if scientists came out and said the age of the Earth was, say, 3.3 billion years.

It is a very different matter to believe in race or capitalism, ideas that we acquired without our knowing it, being almost literally in the air we breathe from the moment we are born and then repeated and affirmed over the years in stories and images and what people say and do. As they become embedded in an expanding web of beliefs, values, experience, and feeling, they acquire so many connections to other parts of our worldview that they can seem to originate from everywhere at once, to have no origin at all but instead to have been for all time, giving them an authority far wider and deeper than that of any particular source. Instead of being the belief of a person, a group, or even a society, they appear as something beyond the reach of mere evidence, opinion, time, or place, not beliefs at all but intuitively true, undeniable, obvious, the way things are, what everybody knows, ordained by God, immutable facts.

So it is that the core principles of white dominance, white identification, and white centeredness have come to be embedded in and indispensable to the mainstream American worldview, along with an almost religious belief in capitalism. This has provided generation after generation of Americans with a lens through which to perceive, interpret, and shape both what is seen to be real and what is imagined to be possible.

Unlike adopting an idea about the age of the Earth, however, we do not decide one day that from now on we are going to believe in race and capitalism. To the extent that we do believe, it is because we grew up with an unquestioned sense of *knowing* it to be so, as something that is second nature and taken for granted as undoubtedly true.

It is an awareness of this kind of 'knowing' that is perhaps the most important thing I have acquired from sociology as a worldview, because it was through this that I came to realize that I even *had* a worldview that I might step back to examine and understand. It is in this way that sociology can provide both a mirror in which to see ourselves in ways we otherwise would not and a window into a larger world, both as it is and what it might become.

Epilogue

Who Are We Really?

On a cool spring evening some years ago, I took a walk down a street I lived on in a small university town. Darkness was just coming on, and only a few people were on the street. As I walked along, I drew closer to a young woman walking in the opposite direction. I had never seen her before, but as we approached each other, I sensed something that startled and perplexed me. And, as my vivid memory of that moment shows, it still troubles me decades later. As we passed each other, she dropped her head, averted her eyes, quickened her step, and veered just a little to one side to widen the gap between us. She seemed to shrink in her body, as if to take up less space. She was, I realized suddenly, afraid of me, walking down this peaceful street on this lovely evening—afraid of me, who hadn't the slightest inclination to do her any harm.

But her reaction had nothing to do with what I intended. It had to do with my belonging to a social category of people—adult males—who are the source of most of the world's violence and almost all the violence and harassment directed at women. That was all she knew about me, and yet apparently this was enough to stir up fear and deference as she moved to hand the sidewalk over to me at that instant of our passing. That wasn't what I wanted, but what I wanted didn't matter, which is the sociological point of the story and the core of my dilemma as an individual.

Social life produces all kinds of consequences, including paths of least resistance that shape how we perceive and think about one another, how we feel, what we do. We are not the paths. They exist in a given situation, regardless of whether we know about them or whether they lead where we would like to go. That I have never been sexually harassing or violent is sociologically irrelevant, because the power and threat that she associated with the status of 'adult male' are rooted in a male-dominated, male-identified, and male-centered world in which we both participated. Since there is no typical violent or harassing male, nothing about me marked me personally as a dangerous individual, but there was also nothing about me that could assure her that I was not. The same was true for her as a potential target, since the characteristic that victims of sexual harassment and violence have most in common is the simple fact of being female. In short, in a patriarchal society, my being male was enough to mark me as a threat, and her being female was enough for her to feel vulnerable to being singled out as a target.

When I realized what was going on, my first reaction was to defend myself. After all, I'm not one of *them*, I thought. I'm Allan the individual, not just a member of some social category. I teach and write and speak about issues of male privilege. I volunteered at a rape crisis service. In a sense, then, I was right, but in another sense, I was quite wrong. My struggle and confusion were over what to make of these categories I belong to, which are most of what many people ever know of me, and certainly all that young woman could know in that moment.

What I came to realize still later was that my insistence on being treated as an individual separate from my place in social systems was a luxury that I could afford in part because of the privilege attached to those same positions. Like many white men, I did not want to think about race or gender or about my being a man and white as significant and problematic in a sexist, racist world. Because if I did, I would have to rethink my comfortable assumptions about how my life was connected to other people's lives through the systems in which we all participate.

When white men complain about affirmative-action programs, for example, they tend to draw attention to issues of individual merit.[1] They are well aware of their own talents and hard work and want to attribute what they get and what they deserve solely to that. What they ignore are the social advantages they have over white women and people of color who are just as talented and work just as hard as they do. They ignore the fact that their success depends in part on the competition being limited by barriers routinely placed in front of them.

People of color, for example, are surrounded by a society in which the path of least resistance is to treat them as invisible, to offer them little encouragement and support in school, and, when all else fails, to openly discriminate against them. And because the white advantage is built into the structure of systems, it does not require open and deliberate discrimination in order to work. In most corporations, for example, the only way to get ahead is to have someone above you notice your potential and act as your mentor and sponsor.[2] Most mentors and sponsors tend to select those they feel most 'comfortable' with—meaning those who are most like them. Since most people who are in a high-enough position to offer mentoring are white, the path of least resistance is to select other whites to bring along.

As long as the promotion process is organized in this way, the advantages that go along with white privilege will continue, even though white people typically do not experience them as such. They will be aware of how hard they have worked to get ahead, so that when a program like affirmative action comes along, they may cry foul at the 'unfair advantages' being given to others. What they do not see are the unfair advantages that are so deeply embedded in how the system is organized that they don't stand out as advantages at all, but simply the way things are normally and appropriately done.

It is hard to sort out who we are in relation to the statuses we occupy, to get a clear sense of some 'real me' that participates in social systems but is also more than that. It is a complexity that holds especially true in societies that place a high value on individualism. We certainly are more than status occupants and role players, but from the moment we are born, just about everything we experience is so entwined with one system or another that the distinction between us and our statuses and roles is hard to make.

I believe, for example, that I have a soul, and that my soul is not a social creation. But the belief itself and all the ways I have available for *thinking* about 'soul'—beginning with the word itself—are rooted in one culture or another. In moments of spiritual practice, I may have experiences that seem separate from the world and social systems. I can have moments in which I seem to stop thinking altogether and sense a reality deeper than words, deeper than thought shaped by culture. But such moments are few and far between, and although they remind me that there is more to human existence than what we know as social life, their fleeting nature also reminds me that social life is what my individual life is about most of the time.

When that young woman and I passed each other on the sidewalk that evening, whatever fear she felt was based on my status as a man in relation to her status as a woman in a world that relates those statuses to each other in particular ways. It was based on a social reality that does not fit many of the ideas I have about myself or how I experience myself. But this doesn't mean that she was reacting to something unreal, because the social reality she and I participated in was every bit as real as the 'real me' and the 'real her' in that moment. Neither of us created that reality, and as individuals, we could do little to change it by ourselves. But it was, whether we liked it or not, connected to who we were and how we saw and acted in relation to each other.

In this way, sociological practice draws us repeatedly to the fact that everything is connected to everything else in one way or another. No experience, no action is complete unto itself. Everything is fundamentally relational. The global economy is about not only nations and flows of capital but also families and communities and neighborhoods and job prospects and stress and arguments over the dinner table and lying awake worrying in the middle of the night. A large-scale problem, such as poverty, is about not only how individuals choose to live but also the systems they participate in that shape the alternatives from which they choose and the paths of least resistance they are encouraged to follow. And something as seemingly simple and unremarkable as two people passing on a sidewalk or having a conversation turns out to be far from it, for it, too, happens in relation to a larger context that shapes its course and gives it meaning.

At every level of social life, the practice of sociology takes us toward a fuller understanding of what is going on and why we feel and act as we do. It provides a foundation for a deeper and clearer awareness of how our lives are connected to these 'things larger than ourselves.'

But the promise of sociology is much greater than that, as the ability to see how social life works becomes a routine part of *how* it works, as sociological thinking becomes a pervasive part of culture itself and the worldview we draw on to construct reality. Sociology then becomes a powerful collective tool in the struggle to understand and do something about the problems that cause so much injustice and unnecessary suffering. It empowers us to look at how we participate in social systems and to see ways to take some small share of responsibility for the consequences that social life produces, to become not only participants in the problem but also part of the solution.

Notes

CHAPTER 1

1. For a classic article on the nature of privilege, see Peggy McIntosh, "White Privilege and Male Privilege: A Personal Account of Coming to See Correspondences through Work in Women's Studies" (Wellesley, MA: Wellesley Centers for Research on Women, 1988).

2. Based on research conducted by Professor Michael Dawson of the University of Chicago, national interviews conducted between October 28 and November 17, 2005.

3. There are, of course, numerous examples of cultures and historical periods where families have behaved in this way, especially in relation to daughters. But in such places as the United States, where organizations are routinely likened to families, this is not how normal family life is viewed.

4. For more on the concept of role conflict, see Erving Goffman, *Encounters* (Indianapolis: Bobbs-Merrill, 1961); Robert K. Merton, *Social Theory and Social Structure*, enl. ed. (New York: Free Press, 1968); and David A. Snow and Leon Anderson, "Identity Work among the Homeless: The Verbal Construction and Avowal of Personal Identities," *American Journal of Sociology* 92, no. 6 (1987): 1336–1371.

5. For a comprehensive summary of findings about the causes of suicide, see David Lester, *Why People Kill Themselves*, 4th ed. (Springfield, IL: Charles C. Thomas, 2000).

6. World Health Organization, Suicide Prevention Programs, January 2007, available at www.who.int/mental_health/prevention/suicide/country_reports/en/index.html; American Foundation for Suicide Prevention, 2013, available at www.afsp.org/understanding-suicide/facts-and-figures.

7. See David Grossman, *On Killing: The Psychological Cost of Learning to Kill in War and Society*, rev. ed. (New York: Back Bay Books, 2009).

8. For more on this way of looking at racism, see David T. Wellman, *Portraits of White Racism*, 2nd ed. (New York: Cambridge University Press, 2012).

9. Harry Brod, "Work Clothes and Leisure Suits: The Class Basis and Bias of the Men's Movement," in *Men's Lives*, ed. Michael S. Kimmel and Michael A. Messner (New York: Macmillan, 1989), 280; emphasis in the original.

10. See, for example, Michele Alexander, *The New Jim* Crow (New York: New Press, 2012); Ellis Cose, *The Rage of a Privileged Class* (New York: HarperCollins, 1993); Joe R. Feagin, "The Continuing Significance of Race. Antiblack Discrimination in Public Places," *American Sociological Review* 56, no. 1 (1991): 101–116; and Joe R. Feagin and Melvin P. Sikes, *Living with Racism. The Black Middle-Class Experience* (Boston: Beacon Press, 1994). See also Eduardo Bonilla-Silva, *Racism without Racists: Color-Blind Racism and the Persistence of Racial Inequality in the United States,* 3rd ed. (Lanham, MD: Rowman and Littlefield, 2009), and Eduardo Bonilla-Silva, *White Supremacy and Racism in the Post–Civil Rights Era* (Boulder, CO. Lynne Rienner, 2001).

11. For useful perspectives on how white people can become more aware of how they are connected to a racist society on a personal level, see Allan G. Johnson, *Privilege, Power, and Difference*, 2nd ed. (New York: McGraw-Hill, 2005), and Paul Kivel, *Uprooting Racism: How White People Can Work for Racial Justice*, 3rd ed. (Philadelphia: New Society, 2011).

CHAPTER 2

1. Susanne K. Langer, "The Growing Center of Knowledge," in *Philosophical Sketches* (Baltimore: Johns Hopkins University Press, 1962), 145–147; emphasis in the original.

2. John Schultz and Todd Gitlin, *No One Was Killed: The Democratic National Convention, August, 1968* (Chicago: University of Chicago Press, 2009).

3. Robert K. Merton, "The Sociology of Social Problems," in *Contemporary Social Problems*, 4th ed., ed. Robert K. Merton and Robert Nisbet (New York: Harcourt Brace Jovanovich, 1976), 22; W. I. Thomas and Dorothy Swain Thomas, *The Child in America* (New York: Knopf, 1928), 572.

4. For sociological critiques of capitalism, just about any text in social stratification will do. See, for example, Richard C. Edwards, Michael Reich, and Thomas E. Weisskopf, eds., *The Capitalist System*, 3rd ed. (Englewood Cliffs, NJ: Prentice-Hall, 1986), and Harold R. Kerbo, *Social Stratification and Inequality: Class Conflict in the United States*, 8th ed. (New York: McGraw-Hill, 2011). See also Jerry Mander, *The Capitalism Papers: Fatal Flaws of an Obsolete System* (Berkeley, CA: Counterpoint Press, 2013), and Richard D. Wolff, *Democracy at Work: A Cure for Capitalism* (Chicago: Haymarket Books, 2012).

5. See James L. Spates, "The Sociology of Values," *Annual Review of Sociology* 9 (1983): 27–49.

6. Quoted in Marvin Harris, *Cultural Materialism* (New York: Random House, 1979), 60.

7. Roger Brown, *Social Psychology* (New York: Free Press, 1965), 407.

8. Émile Durkheim, *Sociology and Philosophy* (1924; repr., New York: Free Press, 1974).

9. See Erving Goffman, *Stigma: Notes on the Management of a Spoiled Identity* (Englewood Cliffs, NJ: Prentice-Hall, 1963).

10. See, for example, Edwin M. Schur, *Labeling Women Deviant: Gender, Stigma, and Social Control* (New York: Random House, 1984).

11. See, for example, Marilyn French, *Beyond Power: On Men, Women, and Morals* (New York: Summit Books, 1985); Carol Brooks Gardner, *Passing By: Gender and Public Harassment* (Berkeley: University of California Press, 1995); National Council for Research on Women, *Sexual Harassment: Research and Resources*, 3rd ed. (New York: National Council for Research on Women, 1995); and Vicki Schultz, "Reconceptualizing Sexual Harassment," *Yale Law Journal* (April 1998): 1683–1805.

12. James Wilson, *The Earth Shall Weep: A History of Native America* (New York: Grove Press, 2001).

13. G. William Domhoff, "Who Rules America?" available at http://whorules america.net/power/wealth.html (updated March 2013). See also Lawrence Mishel and Jared Bernstein, *The State of Working America: 1992–1993* (Armonk, NY: M. E. Sharpe, for Economic Policy Institute, 1993); UN figures reported in the *Los Angeles Times, World Report*, June 14, 1994; Edward N. Wolff, "Recent Trends in Wealth Ownership, 1983–1998," Levy Economics Institute of Bard College, Working Paper 300, April 2000; and World Institute for Development Economics Research of the United Nations University, "Press Release: Pioneering Study Shows Richest Two Percent Own Half World Wealth," New York: Global Policy Forum, December 5, 2006.

14. Although a 2013 U.S. Supreme Court decision invalidated the federal Defense of Marriage Act, thereby granting equal protection to gay and lesbian couples, as of this writing most states continue to discriminate in favor of heterosexual couples.

15. See Gordon W. Allport, "Attitudes," in *A Handbook of Social Psychology*, ed. Charles Murchison (Worcester, MA: Clark University Press, 1935), and K. J. Keicolt, "Recent Developments in Attitudes and Social Structure," *Annual Review of Sociology* 14 (1988): 381–403.

16. See, for example, Henry Abelove, Michele Aina Barale, and David M. Halperin, eds., *The Lesbian and Gay Studies Reader* (New York: Routledge, 1993); Michael S. Kimmel and Michael A. Messner, eds., *Men's Lives*, 9th ed. (New York: Macmillan, 2012); and Suzanne Pharr, *Homophobia: A Weapon of Sexism* (Inverness, CA: Chardon Press, 1988).

17. *New York Times*, April 24, 1983.

18. Michael Parenti, *Inventing Reality*, 2nd ed. (New York: St. Martin's Press, 1993), ch. 2.

19. *Hartford* (CT) *Courant*, April 2, 1989.

20. See Jeffrey D. Clements, *Corporations Are Not People: Why They Have More Rights Than You Do and What You Can Do about It* (San Francisco: Berrett-Koehler Publishers, 2012).

21. Bruce Western and Jake Rosenfeld, "Unions, Norms, and the Rise in U.S. Wage Inequality," *American Sociological Review* 76, no. 4 (2011): 513–537; see also Juliet B. Schor, *The Overworked American: The Unexpected Decline of Leisure* (New York: Basic Books, 1993).

22. See Bill McKibben, *Eaarth: Making a Life on a Tough New Planet* (New York: St. Martins Griffin, 2011).

23. Langer, "Growing Center of Knowledge," 147.

24. See Paul Kivel, *Living in the Shadow of the Cross: Understanding and Resisting the Power and Privilege of Christian Hegemony* (Gabriola Island, Canada: New Society Publishers, 2013).

CHAPTER 3

1. For more on the social significance of time, see R. H. Lauer, *Temporal Man: The Meaning and Uses of Social Time* (New York: Praeger, 1981); Pitirim A. Sorokin and Robert K. Merton, "Social Time: A Methodological and Functional Analysis," *American Journal of Sociology* 42 (1937): 615–629; Eviatar Zerubavel, *Hidden Rhythms: Schedules and Calendars in Social Life* (Chicago: University of Chicago Press, 1981); Eviatar Zerubavel, *The Seven-Day Week: The History and Meaning of the Week* (New York: Free Press, 1985); Barbara Adam, *Timewatch: The Social Analysis of Time* (Cambridge, UK: Polity, 1995); Michael G. Flaherty, *Textures of Time: Agency and Temporal Experience* (Philadelphia: Temple University Press, 2010); and Jay Griffiths, *A Sideways Look at Time* (New York: Tarcher, 2010).

2. For the classic statement on the concept of social structure, see Robert K. Merton, *Social Theory and Social Structure*, enl. ed. (New York: Free Press, 1968).

3. See Jerold Heiss, "Social Roles," in *Social Psychology: Sociological Perspectives*, ed. Morris Rosenberg and Ralph H. Turner (New York: Basic Books, 1981); for the classic statement on the subject, see Ralph Linton, *The Study of Man* (New York: Appleton-Century-Crofts, 1936).

4. This relationship, of course, can also develop between female teachers and male students or between teachers and students of the same sex. But the problems that are the focus of this discussion overwhelmingly occur between male teachers in positions of authority and females who are subordinate to them in some way. See, for example, Center for Research on Women, *Secrets in Public: Sexual Harassment in Our Schools* (Wellesley, MA: Wellesley College Center for Research on Women, 1993); Billie Wright Dziech and Linda Weiner, *The Lecherous Professor: Sexual Harassment on Campus* (Boston: Beacon Press, 1984); and Michele A. Paludi and L. A. Strayer, *Ivory Power: Sexual Harassment on Campus* (Albany: State University of New York Press, 1990).

5. See, for example, Joan Abramson, *Old Boys—New Women: Sexual Harassment in the Workplace* (New York: Praeger, 1993); Center for Research on Women, *Secrets in Public*; Dziech and Weiner, *Lecherous Professor*; Carol Brooks Gardner, *Passing By: Gender and Public Harassment* (Berkeley: University of California Press, 1995); Barbara A. Gutek, *Sex and the Workplace: The Impact of Sexual Behavior and Harassment on Women, Men, and Organizations* (San Francisco: Jossey-Bass, 1985); Catharine A. MacKinnon, *Sexual Harassment of Working Women: A Case of Sex Discrimination* (New Haven, CT: Yale University Press, 1979); and Paludi and Strayer, *Ivory Power*.

6. See, for example, Susan Brownmiller, *Against Our Will: Men, Women, and Rape* (New York: Simon and Schuster, 1975); David Finkelhor and Kersti Yllo, *License to Rape: Sexual Abuse of Wives* (New York: Holt, Rinehart, and Winston, 1985); Michael A. Messner and Donald F. Sabo, *Sex, Violence, and Power in Sports: Rethinking*

Masculinity (Freedom, CA: Crossing Press, 1994); Myriam Miedzian, *Boys Will Be Boys: Breaking the Link between Violence and Masculinity* (New York: Doubleday, 1991); Diana E. H. Russell, *Sexual Exploitation: Rape, Child Sexual Abuse, and Workplace Harassment* (Beverly Hills, CA: Sage, 1984); Peggy Reeves Sanday, *A Woman Scorned: Acquaintance Rape on Trial* (New York: Doubleday, 1996); and Patricia Searles and Ronald J. Berger, eds., *Rape and Society* (Boulder, CO: Westview Press, 1995).

7. Robert K. Merton, "Social Structure and Anomie," *American Sociological Review* 3 (1938): 672–682.

8. D. Jacobs, "Inequality and Economic Crime," *Sociology and Social Research* 66, no. 1 (1981): 12–28.

9. Gallup Poll, June 9–11, 2011, available at www.gallup.com/poll/148187/Americans-Prefer-Boys-Girls-1941.aspx.

10. Robert E. Kennedy Jr., "The Social Status of the Sexes and Their Relative Mortality in Ireland," in *Readings in Population*, ed. William Petersen (New York: Macmillan, 1972), 121–135.

11. For more on this subject, see Carl N. Degler, *At Odds: Women and the Family in America from the Revolution to the Present* (New York: Oxford University Press, 1980); Robert L. Griswold, *Fatherhood in America: A History* (New York: Basic Books, 1993); and Eli Zaretsky, *Capitalism, the Family, and Personal Life*, rev. and exp. ed. (New York: Harper and Row, 1986).

12. See Heidi Hartmann, "The Unhappy Marriage of Marxism and Feminism: Towards a More Progressive Union," in *Women and Revolution: A Discussion of the Unhappy Marriage of Marxism and Feminism*, ed. Lydia Sargent (Boston: South End Press, 1981), 1–41, and Martha May, "Bread before Roses: American Workingmen, Labor Unions, and the Family Wage," in *Women, Work, and Protest*, ed. Ruth Milkman (Boston: Routledge and Kegan Paul, 1985).

13. See Viviana A. Zelizer, *Pricing the Priceless Child: The Changing Social Value of Children* (New York: Basic Books, 1985).

14. Margaret Mead, *Coming of Age in Samoa* (1928; repr., New York: Modern Library, 1953).

15. See E. Anthony Rotundo, *American Manhood: Transformations in Masculinity from the Revolution to the Modern Era* (New York: Basic Books, 1993).

16. U.S. Census Bureau, *Statistical Abstract of the United States: 2012* (Washington, DC: U.S. Government Printing Office, 2013), table 59.

17. For a clear look at racism in both its cultural and structural aspects, see David T. Wellman, *Portraits of White Racism*, 2nd ed. (New York: Cambridge University Press, 2012).

18. William H. Frey, "Census Data: Blacks and Hispanics Take Different Segregation Paths" (Washington, DC: Brookings Institution, 2010), available at www.brookings.edu/research/opinions/2010/12/16-census-frey; Reynolds Farley and William H. Frey, "Changes in the Segregation of Whites from Blacks during the 1980s," *American Sociological Review* 59 (1994); Douglas S. Massey and Nancy A. Denton, *American Apartheid: Segregation and the Making of the Underclass* (Cambridge, MA: Harvard University Press, 1998).

19. See Lee Sigelman and S. Welch, "The Contact Hypothesis Revisited: Black-White Interaction and Positive Racial Attitudes," *Social Forces* 71, no. 3 (1993): 781–795.

20. Pew Research Center, *A Survey of LGBT Americans: Attitudes, Experiences, and Values in Changing Times* (Washington, DC: Pew Research Center, 2013); Pew Research Center, *In Gay Marriage Debate, Both Supporters and Opponents See Legal Recognition as "Inevitable"* (Washington, DC: Pew Research Center, 2013).

21. Gunnar Myrdal, *An American Dilemma* (New York. Harper and Row, 1945).

22. Karl Marx, *Capital: A Critique of Political Economy* (1987; repr., New York; International Publishers, 1975).

23. David R. Francis, "The Economic Expansion Is Finally Paying Off for Most Americans," *Christian Science Monitor*, online edition, September 27, 1996, available at www.csmonitor.com.

24. U.S. Census Bureau, *Statistical Abstract of the United States: 2012* (Washington, DC: U.S. Census Bureau, 2013), table 690.

25. See Gretchen Morgensen and Joshua Rosner, *Reckless Endangerment: How Outsized Ambition, Greed, and Corruption Created the Worst Financial Crisis of Our Time* (New York: Times Books, 2011).

CHAPTER 4

1. For some fundamental statements, see Amos H. Hawley, *Human Ecology: A Theoretical Essay* (Chicago: University of Chicago Press, 1986); Michael Micklin and Harvey M. Choldin, eds., *Sociological Human Ecology: Contemporary Issues and Applications* (Boulder, CO: Westview Press, 1984); and Gerhard Lenski and Patrick Nolan, *Human Societies: An Introduction to Macrosociology*, 11th ed. (New York: Oxford, 2010).

2. Virginia Woolf, *A Room of One's Own* (New York: Harcourt, Brace and World, 1929).

3. The classic work on the social uses of space is Robert Sommer, *Personal Space: The Behavioral Analysis of Design* (Englewood Cliffs, NJ: Prentice-Hall, 1969).

4. See Donald S. Massey and Nancy A. Denton, *American Apartheid: Segregation and the Making of the Underclass*, (Cambridge, MA: Harvard University Press, 1998).

5. For a fascinating novel that examines human beings as an 'exceptional' species, see Daniel Quinn, *Ishmael* (New York: Bantam, 1992).

6. Marvin Harris, *Cows, Pigs, Wars, and Witches* (New York: Random House, 1974). See also his *Cannibals and Kings: The Origins of Cultures* (New York: Random House, 1977); *Cultural Materialism* (New York: Random House, 1979); and *Good Things to Eat: Riddles of Food and Culture* (New York: Simon and Schuster, 1985). For an introduction to sociology that uses an ecological approach, see Patrick Nolan and Gerhard E. Lenski, *Human Societies*, 10th ed. (New York: Paradigm, 2005).

7. Gerhard Lenski, *Power and Privilege: A Theory of Social Stratification* (Chapel Hill: University of North Carolina Press, 1984).

8. Population Reference Bureau, "2012 World Population Data Sheet" (Washington, DC: Population Reference Bureau, 2013).

9. From U.S. Census Bureau data, reported on NBCnews.com, June 13, 2013, available at http://usnews.nbcnews.com/_news/2013/06/13/18934111-census-white-majority-in-us-gone-by-2043?lite.

10. U.S. Census Bureau, "World Population Information" and "International Data

Base," available at www.census.gov/ipc/www/ world.html; Population Reference Bureau, "2012 World Population Data Sheet" (Washington, DC: Population Reference Bureau, 2013).

11. See B. P. Dohrenwend and B. S. Dohrenwend, "Sex Differences in Psychiatric Disorders," *American Journal of Sociology* 81 (1976): 1447–1454, and Lois Verbrugge and D. L. Wingard, "Sex Differentials in Health and Mortality," *Women and Health* 12, no. 2 (1987). See also Nicholas R. Eaton, Robert. F. Krueger, Katherine M. Keyes, Deborah S. Hasin, Steve Balsis, Andrew E. Skodol, Kristian E. Markon, Bridget F. Grant, "An Invariant Dimensional Liability Model of Gender Differences in Mental Disorder Prevalence: Evidence from a National Sample," *Journal of Abnormal Psychology, Online First*, August 17, 2011, available at www.apa.org/pubs/journals/releases/abn-ofp-eaton.pdf.

12. From data gathered regularly by the University of Chicago National Opinion Research Center, General Social Surveys.

13. A. M. Miniño, M. P. Heron, and B. L. Smith, "Deaths: Preliminary Data for 2004," *National Vital Statistics Reports* 54, no. 19 (Hyattsville, MD: National Center for Health Statistics, 2006); U.S. Census Bureau, *Statistical Abstract of the United States: 2012* (Washington, DC: U.S. Census Bureau, 2013).

14. U.S. Census Bureau, *Statistical Abstract: 2012*; Lester R. Brown, *Plan B3.0: Mobilizing to Save Civilization*, rev. ed. (New York: Norton, 2008); William R. Cline, *Global Warming and Agriculture: Estimates by Country* (Washington, DC: Petersen Institute, 2007).

15. U.S. Census Bureau, "World Population Information" and "International Data Base"; Population Reference Bureau, "2012 World Population Data Sheet."

16. International Energy Agency, World Energy Outlook 2012, Executive Summary (Paris: International Energy Agency, 2012).

CHAPTER 5

1. See, for example, B. F. Skinner, *Beyond Freedom and Dignity* (New York: Knopf, 1971).

2. For more on the concept of the self, see D. H. Demo, "The Self-Concept over Time: Research Issues and Directions," *Annual Review of Sociology* 18 (1992): 303–326, and Morris Rosenberg, *Conceiving the Self* (New York: Basic Books, 1979).

3. George Herbert Mead, *Mind, Self, and Society* (Chicago: University of Chicago Press, 1934).

4. Erving Goffman, *Encounters* (Indianapolis: Bobbs-Merrill, 1961).

5. 'Significant others' is a term first introduced in Harry Stack Sullivan, *The Interpersonal Theory of Psychiatry* (New York: Norton, 1953).

6. Charles Horton Cooley, *Life and the Student* (New York: Knopf, 1927).

7. Mead, *Mind, Self, and Society*.

8. See the following works by Erving Goffman: *The Presentation of Self in Everyday Life* (New York: Doubleday, 1959); *Asylums* (New York: Anchor Books, 1961); *Behavior in Public Places* (New York: Free Press, 1963); *Stigma: Notes on the Management of a Spoiled Identity* (Englewood Cliffs, NJ: Prentice-Hall, 1963); *Interaction Ritual* (New

York: Anchor Books, 1967); *Gender Advertisements* (New York: Harper Colophon, 1976); *Forms of Talk* (Philadelphia: University of Pennsylvania Press, 1981); and *Encounters*. See also Philip Manning, *Erving Goffman and Modern Sociology* (Stanford, CA; Stanford University Press, 1992).

9. Erving Goffman, "Embarrassment and Social Organization," *American Journal of Sociology* 62 (1956–1957): 264–271.

10. The study of methods people use to sustain the reality of a particular situation is known as 'ethnomethodology' (literally, 'people's methods'). It is most closely associated with the work of Harold Garfinkel. See his *Studies in Ethnomethodology* (Englewood Cliffs, NJ: Prentice-Hall, 1967). See also J. Maxwell Atkinson and John Heritage, *Structures of Social Action: Studies in Conversation Analysis* (Cambridge, UK: Cambridge University Press, 1984); R. A. Hilbert, "Ethnomethodology and the Micro-Macro-Order," *American Sociological Review* 55, no. 6 (1990): 794–808; and Eric Livingston, *Making Sense of Ethnomethodology* (London: Routledge and Kegan Paul, 1987).

11. See Goffman, *Interaction Ritual*.

12. See, for example, the following works by Deborah Tannen: *You Just Don't Understand: Women and Men in Conversation* (New York: William Morrow, 1990) and *Talking Nine to Five* (New York: William Morrow, 1994).

13. Rosabeth Moss Kanter, *Men and Women of the Corporation* (New York: Basic Books, 1977).

14. See Brian McNaught, *Gay Issues in the Workplace* (New York: St. Martin's Press, 1993).

15. For more on the concept of privilege, see Peggy McIntosh, "White Privilege and Male Privilege: A Personal Account of Coming to See Correspondences through Work in Women's Studies" (Wellesley, MA: Wellesley Centers for Research on Women, 1988).

16. Such stories abound in the experiences of people of color in the United States. See, for example, Lois Benjamin, *The Black Elite* (Chicago: Nelson-Hall, 1991); Ellis Cose, *The Rage of a Privileged Class* (New York: HarperCollins, 1993); Joe R. Feagin, "The Continuing Significance of Race: Antiblack Discrimination in Public Places," *American Sociological Review* 56, no. 1 (1991): 101–116; Joe R. Feagin, Hernán Vera, and Pinar Batur, *White Racism: The Basics* (New York: Routledge, 1995); Joe R. Feagin, Hernán Vera, and Nikitah Imani, *The Agony of Education: Black Students at White Colleges and Universities* (New York: Routledge, 1996); Joe R. Feagin and Melvin P. Sikes, *Living with Racism: The Black Middle-Class Experience* (Boston: Beacon Press, 1994); and David T. Wellman, *Portraits of White Racism*, 2nd ed. (New York: Cambridge University Press, 2012).

CHAPTER 6

1. For the classic statement on the norm of reciprocity, see Alvin W. Gouldner, "A Norm of Reciprocity: A Preliminary Statement," *American Sociological Review* 25 (1960): 161–178. See also Marcel Mauss, *The Gift* (1925; repr., New York: Free Press, 1954). For more on exchange theory, see Peter M. Blau, *Exchange and Power in Social Life* (New York: Wiley, 1986), and K. S. Cook, ed., *Social Exchange Theory* (Newbury Park, CA: Sage, 1987).

2. Howard Steven Friedman. *The Measure of a Nation: How to Regain America's Competitive Edge and Boost Our Global Standing* (Amherst, NY: Prometheus Books, 2012).

3. Nate Silver, "Measuring the Effects of Voter Identification Laws," *New York Times*, June 15, 2012.

4. John Kenneth Galbraith, "Why the Welfare State Is Here to Stay," interview by Nathan Gardells, *National Times*, June 1996, 30.

5. Ibid.

6. See Erik J. Engstrom, *Partisan Gerrymandering and the Construction of American Democracy* (Ann Arbor: University of Michigan Press, 2013).

7. For a classic statement of this principle, see Robert K. Merton, "The Sociology of Social Problems," in *Contemporary Social Problems*, 4th ed., ed. Robert K. Merton and Robert Nisbet (New York: Harcourt Brace Jovanovich, 1976), 5–43.

8. U.S. Census Bureau, *Statistical Abstract of the United States: 2012* (Washington, DC: U.S. Government Printing Office, 2012).

9. See William Julius Wilson, *When Work Disappears: The World of the New Urban Poor* (New York: Knopf, 1996).

10. Charles Murray, *Losing Ground* (New York: Basic Books, 1984).

11. Ibid., 221.

12. Ibid., 227–228.

13. Ibid., 233.

14. U.S. Census Bureau, *Statistical Abstract of the United States, 2012* (Washington, DC: U.S. Government Printing Office, 2012), table 694.

15. Emmanuel Saez, "Striking It Richer: The Evolution of Top Incomes in the United States," Stanford Center for the Study of Poverty and Inequality, *Pathways Magazine* (Winter 2008): 6–7.

16. Lydia DePillis, "Congrats CEOs! You're Making 273 Times the Pay of the Average Worker," *Washington Post*, June 26, 2013, available at www.washingtonpost.com/blogs/wonkblog/wp/2013/06/26/congrats-ceos-youre-making-273-times-the-pay-of-the-average-worker/.

17. For international comparisons that illustrate alternatives to how things are done in the United States, see David Brady, *Rich Democracies, Poor People: How Politics Explain Poverty* (New York: Oxford, 2009).

18. Associated Press, "U.S. Majority Have Prejudice against Blacks," *USA Today*, October 27, 2012.

19. See Jackson Katz, *Leading Men: Presidential Campaigns and the Politics of Manhood* (Northampton, MA: Interlink, 2012).

20. Richard Slotkin, *Regeneration through Violence: The Mythology of the American Frontier, 1600–1860* (Norman: University of Oklahoma Press, 2000); Richard Slotkin, *The Fatal Environment: The Myth of the Frontier in the Age of Industrialization, 1800–1890* (Norman: University of Oklahoma Press, 1998); Richard Slotkin, *Gunfighter Nation: Myth of the American Frontier in Twentieth-Century America* (Norman: University of Oklahoma Press, 1998).

21. See Stephen Kinzer, *Overthrow: America's Century of Regime Change from Hawaii to Iraq* (New York: Times Books, 2007).

22. See Richard Slotkin, *Gunfighter Nation*.

23. See, for example, Karen DeYoung and Scott Clement, "Americans Say Afghan War Not Worth Fighting," *Washington Post,* July 26, 2013, and Pew Research Center, "Veterans of Post-9/11 Wars Ambivalent about Whether Iraq Was Worth It," March 19, 2013, available at www.pewresearch.org/daily-number/veterans-of-post-911-wars-ambivalent-about-whether-iraq-was-worth-it/.

CHAPTER 7

1. See Theodore W. Allen, *The Invention of the White Race*, vols. 1–2, 2nd ed. (New York: Verso, 2012), and Audrey Smedley and Brian Smedley, *Race in North America: Origin and Evolution of a Worldview*, 4th ed. (Boulder, CO: Westview Press, 2011).

2. See Smedley, *Race in North America*. See also Dee Brown, *Bury My Heart at Wounded Knee. An Indian History of the American West*, 30th anniv. ed. (New York: Owl Books, 2001).

3. For a history of this transition, see Basil Davidson, *The African Slave Trade* (Boston: Back Bay Books, 1988).

4. For more on this history, see James R. Barrett and David R. Roediger, "How White People Became White," in *Critical White Studies,* ed. Richard Delgado and Jean Stefancic (Philadelphia: Temple University Press, 1997), 402–406, and David R. Roediger, *The Wages of Whiteness: Race and the Making of the American Working Class,* rev. ed. (New York: Verso, 2007).

5. See George Lipsitz, *The Possessive Investment in Whiteness: How White People Profit from Identity Politics,* rev. and enl. ed. (Philadelphia: Temple University Press, 2006).

6. William H. Chafe, *Civilities and Civil Rights: Greensboro, North Carolina and the Black Struggle for Freedom* (New York: Oxford University Press, 1981).

EPILOGUE

1. On affirmative action, see Paul Kivel, *Uprooting Racism: How White People Can Work for Racial Justice,* 3rd ed. (Philadelphia: New Society, 2011), 172–179; Nicolaus Mills, ed., *Debating Affirmative Action* (New York: Dell, 1994); and David T. Wellman, *Portraits of White Racism,* 2nd ed. (New York: Cambridge University Press, 2012), 226–236.

2. See R. Roosevelt Thomas Jr., *Beyond Race and Gender* (New York: AMACOM, 1991).

Glossary

Words in italics refer to entries included elsewhere in the glossary.

achieved status. Also known as an *acquired status*, a position in a *social system* that is occupied after birth, such as marital *status*, educational level, and occupation.

acquired status. See *achieved status*.

action. A *behavior* that takes into account a consideration of how other people will interpret and respond to it.

agricultural society. A society in which economic activity centers on the production of food through the cultivation of large fields, usually involving the use of a plow or its equivalent.

attitude. A positive or negative evaluation of people, objects, or situations that predisposes those who hold it to feel and therefore behave in positive or negative ways.

behavior. Anything a person does.

belief. A statement about reality or about what is regarded as true or false.

boundary. The rules and understandings that govern who may occupy a particular *social status*.

bureaucracy. A complex *social system* consisting of formal relationships among *status* occupants who specialize in narrowly defined tasks governed by rigid rules and a clear hierarchy. Managers specialize in making sure that rules are followed and that decisions are based on rational consideration of the organization's best interests rather than the personal feelings of individuals.

capitalism. An *economic system* in which the *means of production* are privately owned by some (capitalists and investors) but used by others (workers) who sell their time in return for wages and produce goods and services.

class. See *social class*.

coalition. A subgroup in which members join forces to control what goes on in the *group*.

colonialism. An international *system* of economic dominance through which more *powerful* nations exploit weaker ones.

conflict perspective. A *sociological* perspective that focuses on how groups and individuals struggle with one another over resources and rewards, resulting in particular distributions of wealth, *power*, and prestige in *societies* and other *social systems*. These conflicts shape not only the patterns of everyday life but also larger patterns, such as *racial*, ethnic, *gender*, and *social class* inequality and relations among *societies* and regions of the world.

contradiction. An instance in which two or more aspects of a *social system* are incompatible or in conflict with each other, often producing tension leading to change.

cultural materialism. A *sociological* perspective that focuses on the ways in which material conditions in a *social system*, such as climate, shape *cultural beliefs, values, attitudes,* and *norms*.

culture. The accumulated store of *symbols*, ideas, and material objects associated with a *social system*.

deviance. Any instance in which a *norm* is violated.

division of labor. A structural feature of *social systems* in which a process, such as producing goods or raising a family, is divided into various tasks that are assigned to the occupants of different *social statuses*.

dramaturgical perspective. A *sociological* perspective that takes the point of view that social interaction is like a theatrical performance that can be understood in terms of scripts, players, *roles*, and audiences.

ecology. The study of the relationship between *social systems* and physical environments.

economic system. A set of institutional arrangements through which goods and services are produced and distributed in a *society*.

ecosystem. A natural *system* in which forms of life live in relation to one another in a shared physical environment.

ethnocentrism. The tendency to view the ideas and practices of other *cultures* as inferior or incorrect.

ethnomethodology. The study of the unspoken rules and meanings that people use to interpret one another's *behavior* and form expectations in social situations.

functional perspective. A theoretical perspective in *sociology* that focuses on the ways in which *cultural* ideas and *social structures* contribute to or interfere with the maintenance or adaptation of a *social system*.

gender. A collection of *cultural* ideas used to construct images and expectations associated with the biological categories of female and male (such as 'women,' 'men,' 'manhood').

generalized other. The shared perception of the ideas and expectations that apply to people who occupy a particular *social status* in a social situation (e.g., customer in a store, passenger on a bus).

gerrymandering. A legislative process through which electoral districts are redrawn so as to advantage the political party in *power* by increasing the number of districts where they hold a majority.

gesture. A physical movement (such as waving your hand) that in a particular *culture* has meaning.

group. A *social system* involving two or more people who interact with one another in regular and patterned ways and identify one another as members (e.g., a family or basketball team).

horticultural society. A *society* that organizes the *economic system* primarily around the cultivation of small gardens using digging sticks and hoes.

hunter-gatherer society. A *society* that organizes the *economic system* around hunting for game and gathering vegetable foodstuffs.

ideology. A set of *cultural* ideas used to explain and justify the status quo or movements for social change.

individualism. A way of thinking based on the idea that everything that happens in social life results solely from the thoughts and feelings of individuals without reference to their participation in *social systems*.

industrial society. A *society* that organizes the *economic system* around the centralized production of goods using machinery and nonanimal sources of *power*.

interaction ritual. Rituals performed as part of social interaction to sustain the shared reality of a particular social situation or relationship (such as greeting people you meet on the street and asking how they are).

LGBT. An acronym standing for 'lesbian,' 'gay,' 'bisexual,' and '*transgender.*' Some activists add the letter 'Q' for '*queer,*' as in 'LGBTQ.'

looking-glass self. Our perception of ourselves based on how we think other people perceive and evaluate us.

luxury of obliviousness. An aspect of *systems* of *privilege* by which members of dominant groups have the option of choosing whether to be aware of the true extent, causes, and consequences of *privilege* and *oppression*.

male centeredness. An organizing principle of *patriarchy* by which the *path of least resistance* is always to place males and what they do at the center of attention.

male dominance. An organizing principle of *patriarchy* by which the default condition is for men to hold positions of *power*.

male identification. An organizing principle of *patriarchy* by which males are taken to be the standard for human beings and are thereby regarded as superior to females.

Manifest Destiny. Originating in the nineteenth century, Manifest Destiny was an *ideology* by which the United States was chosen by God to expand across the continent and spread its influence and *culture* to 'uncivilized' peoples in other parts of the world.

material culture. Objects made by people as they participate in *social systems* and interact with one another and the physical environment.

means of production. Tools, machines, resources, and technology used in an *economic system* to produce goods and services.

migration. The movement of people from one place to another.

mode of production. The way in which a *society* organizes the production of goods and services (e.g., *agricultural*, *industrial*).

norm. A social rule of appearance or *behavior* that links *beliefs* and *values* to rewards and/or punishments.

oppression. In a *social system*, the subordination, exploitation, and mistreatment of one *social category* by another as an assertion of *privilege*.

overpopulation. A condition in which population size outstrips available resources, within a *social system*, regionally, or globally.

path of least resistance. In a *social system*, the path of least resistance in a particular situation consists of whatever *behavior* or appearance is expected of participants depending on their position in that system.

patriarchy. A *social system* organized around the principles of *male dominance, male centeredness, male identification*, and an obsession with control that is *gendered* as masculine.

performative language. An act of speech that alters the terms of a social relationship (as in saying, "I promise").

population. A collection of people who share a geographic territory or participate in a *social system*.

post-industrial society. A *society* whose *economic system* is organized more around the providing of services than the production of goods.

power. The ability to have an effect, including the assertion of control and dominance, in spite of opposition.

power structure. The distribution of *power* in a *social system*.

prejudice. A positive or negative *attitude* directed at people simply because they occupy a particular *social status*.

privilege. An advantage that is unearned, exclusive to a particular *social category*, and socially conferred by others.

queer. A general term used by some *LGBT* activists for those who, in various ways, reject, test, or otherwise transgress the boundaries of what is culturally regarded as normal in relation to *gender*, gender identity, or sexual orientation and expression.

race. A set of *cultural* categories based on the scientifically groundless assumption that different kinds of human beings exist, as indicated by such physical characteristics as skin color, hair texture, and facial features.

racism. A broad category that includes anything having the effect of enacting, enforcing, or perpetuating a *system* of *privilege* based on *race*.

reality. See *social construction of reality*.

reciprocity, norm of. A social expectation that an *action* will be responded to in a mutual and appropriate way that sustains a relationship (such as responding to what someone says in a conversation or returning a favor).

role. A set of *beliefs, values, norms*, and *attitudes* associated with a *social status* in a *social system* that shapes how people participate in and experience social life in relation to the occupants of other statuses (as in the role of 'wife' in relation to 'husband').

role conflict. An instance in which the expectations or ideas attached to one *role* conflict with those attached to another.

role structure. The arrangement of *social statuses* in a *system* and their corresponding *roles*.

segregation. The enforced physical separation of members of different *social categories* from one another.

sexism. Anything that has as a consequence the enactment or perpetuation of *privilege* based on *gender*.

significant other. In social relationships, a particular individual whose expectations, judgments, and *behavior* affect our behavior, experience, and perception of ourselves.

situational status. A *social status* occupied only through participation in a particular situation (such as being an airline passenger) and no longer occupied once that participation ends.

social category. The collection of all people who occupy a particular *social status* (e.g, 'college students' or 'white people').

social class. In general, distinctions and divisions resulting from the unequal distribution of resources and rewards, such as wealth or *power*, in a *social system*. A Marxist approach focuses on how relationships among capitalists, workers, and the *means of production* produce inequality. More mainstream approaches focus on people's ability to satisfy wants and needs, especially through income and the use of prestige and *power*.

social construction of reality. The social process of interaction using language and other *symbols* through which people's perceptions of what is considered to be real are constructed and shared.

social identity. The sum total of who we think we are in relation to other people and *social systems*.

socialization. The process through which people are prepared to perform *roles* that go with particular *social* statuses and otherwise participate in a *social system*.

social status. A position that people may occupy in a *social system* that locates them in relation to the occupants of other statuses (e.g., parent-child).

social structure. The patterns of relationships and distributions that characterize the organization of a *social system*. Relationships connect various elements of a *system* (such as *social statuses*) to one another and to the system itself. Distributions include *valued* resources and rewards, such as *power* and income, and the distribution of people among social statuses. Structure can also refer to relationships and distributions among systems.

social system. An interconnected collection of *social structural* relationships, *ecological* arrangements, *cultural symbols*, ideas, objects, and *population* dynamics and conditions that combine to form a whole. Complex systems comprise smaller systems that are related to one another and the larger system through cultural, structural, ecological, and population arrangements and dynamics.

society. A *social system* defined by a particular territory, within which a population shares a common *culture* and way of life under conditions of relative autonomy, independence, and self-sufficiency. It is also the largest such system for which members of the population identify themselves as members.

sociology. The systematic study of social life and *behavior*, especially in relation to *social systems*, how they work, how they change, their complex relation to people's lives, and the consequences that result.

state. The social institution that is granted a monopoly over the legitimate use of force.

status. See *social status*.

stereotype. A rigid, oversimplified *belief* that is attached to all members of a particular *group* or *social category*.

stigma. Personal characteristics (such as physical appearance) that are in themselves regarded by others as violations of a *norm* and therefore a form of *deviance*.

symbol. Objects, characteristics of objects (e.g., color), *gestures*, or words that represent more than themselves in a particular *culture*.

system. See *social system.*

time structure. In a *social system*, the ways in which social relationships are defined, conditioned, and regulated by time.

transgender. A transgender person is someone whose internal experience of *gender* does not match the sex assigned at birth.

value. An idea about relative worth, goodness, or desirability used to make choices among different alternatives. In a *patriarchy*, for example, maleness is *culturally* valued above femaleness, and being in control is valued above not being in control.

worldview. The collection of interconnected *beliefs, values, attitudes*, images, stories, and memories out of which a sense of reality is constructed and maintained in a *social system* and in the minds of individuals who participate in it.

Index

Main entries in bold are included in the Glossary.

abolitionist movement, 152–153
abuse in families, causes of, 70–71. *See also* violence
achieved status, 67
action, 113–114
adolescence as life stage, 80
affirmative action, 137, 152, 162–163
Afghanistan, war in, 145
Africa, population growth in, 104
agricultural societies, 98, 99; race and, 150
American Dilemma, An, 85
American Indians. *See* Native Americans
Amos 'n' Andy, 14, 23
antipoverty programs, 136–137, 139–140
Apple, 21
ascribed status, 67
attitudes, cultural, 50–53
Aurora, Colorado, mass murders in, 142. *See also* mass murder
authenticity of self, 115–116
automation, 58

behavior, 113
beliefs, cultural, 37–39
Bill of Rights, race and, 151
bin Laden, Osama, 144–145

birth rate, 95, 100–101, 105
boundaries, community, 90; and inequality, 46, 47–48; norms, deviance, and, 47–48; performative language and, 129
Britain. *See* Great Britain
Brod, Harry, 23
Brown, Roger, 43
bureaucracy, 78, 100
Bush, George W., 8

capitalism: contradictions of, 86–87; criticism of, 39, 56–57; and democracy, 39; efficiency and, 58; and families, 79–83; men and, 81–83; as mode of production, 98; poverty and, 135–136; racism and, 150–153; as a social system, 86–87; state and, 87–88; women and, 80, 81–83
Canada, voting in, 131
child care as women's work, 80, 82
children in family role structures, 79–81, 88
China: bureaucracy in, 100; Internet control in, 59; status of women in, 78; working conditions in, 21
Christianity, ethnocentrism and, 61
cities, crisis in inner, 89–90. *See also* urbanization

Citizens United v. Federal Elections Commission, 56
civil rights movement, 85–86, 155–156
climate change, 59, 95, 104, 149
Clinton, Bill, 66–67
coalitions, 76, 101–102
colonialism, 99
community **boundaries.** *See* boundaries, community
computers as material culture, 57–58
conflict perspective, 48–50
Congress, ecology of U.S., 93–94
conservative approach to poverty, 136–139, 140–141
Constitution, race and U.S., 151
contradictions, role of in social life, 72, 151, 85–86. *See also* capitalism
conversations, sustaining, 119–120
corporations as social systems, 13, 165n3
cows as sacred in Hindu religion, 95–96
crime: ecology and, 94; opportunity structure and, 72–74
cultural **attitudes**, 50–53
cultural **beliefs**, 37–39
cultural materialism, 95–96
cultural **norms.** *See* norms, cultural
cultural **values.** *See* values, cultural
culture, 31–62; individuals' relation to, 42–44, 117–118; material, 54–60; and the social construction of reality, 33–37; and social structure, 83–88, 152. *See also* cultural materialism, 95–96; language; norms; values, cultural
Custer's Last Stand, 144
cyberspace, 58–59, 94

death, patterns of, 18–20, 100–101, 103–104
democracy, **capitalism** and, 39
Democratic Party, 132; 1968 Democratic presidential convention, 36–37
deviance: innovative, 73; morality, boundaries and, 47–48; opportunity structure and, 72–74; types of, 73
distributions, structural, 26, 27, 35, 39, 55, 65, 72–73, 77–78, 83, 85, 90, 94, 102, 135, 137, 149, 155, 156
diversity training, 7–8
division of labor, 100
divorce: changing views of, 85; poverty and, 136

dramaturgical perspective, 114–117
Durkheim, Émile, 18, 47

ecological niches, 98
ecology, 93–98; race and, 94, 150–151; voting and, 133–134. *See also* segregation, racial
economic efficiency, 58, 86–87, 135
economic system, family and, 79–83
ecosystems, 94–95
educational attainment, death rates and, 103
efficiency, economic, 58, 86–87, 135
Egypt, Internet control in, 59
embarrassment, 115
emotional detachment as cultural attitude, 52–53
energy use, population and, 105
England. *See* Great Britain
Enlightenment, Age of, 9–10
ethnocentrism, 60–62
ethnomethodology, 119–121, 172n10
Europe, election of parliaments in, 132

family: abuse in, 70–71; and economy, 77–83; family wage, 80; historical changes in, 79–83; population dynamics in, 101–102; power structures in, 79, 102; role structure in, 75–76, 88, 102; as social system, 12, 70; strain in, 88–89
Federal Housing Authority (FHA), 154
freedom, 42
freedom of press, 55–56
Freud, Sigmund, 10
functional perspective, 46–48

Galbraith, John Kenneth, 133
gender: death rates and, 103; emotion and, 53; and families, 79–83; gender inequality, 77–78, 122–123; gender preference for births, 77; gender pronouns, 34–35; language and, 33–35; sexual harassment and, 68–70, 161, 168n4; suicide and, 18; talk and, 121–122; violence and, 70–72, 141–146; work and, 80–83. *See also* family; men; patriarchy; women
generalized other, 111–113
genocide, 150, 151, 154
gerrymandering, 133
global warming, 59, 95, 104, 149
God, cultural idea of, 37
Goffman, Erving, 110, 114–117

government: and contradictions of capitalism, 87–88; control of information by, 55, 58–59

Great Britain: ideas about property of, 49; origins of white privilege and, 150–151; subjugation of Ireland by, 150; worldview of, 150, 151, 152

Greensboro, North Carolina, racial segregation in, 155–156

Gutenberg, Johannes, 55

Harold and Maude, 129–130

Harris, Marvin, 95–96

health care reform, 66–67

heterosexism, 50–51, 122–123, 167n14. *See also* gender; patriarchy; sexual orientation

Hinduism and sacred status of cows, 95–96

Ho-Chunk tribe, 153

homosexuality, cultural beliefs about, 37, 50. *See also* gender; patriarchy; sexual orientation

horticultural societies, 98, 99

House of Commons of Great Britain, ecology of, 94

Hungary, suicide rate in, 19

hunter-gatherer societies, 98, 99

immigration, illegal, 100–101

impression management, 114–115, 116–117

income: death rates and, 103; distribution of in United States, 86–87, 137–138, 139

India: energy use in, 105; and Hindu religion, 95–96; population growth in, 104

individualism, 9–12, 17–21, 24–26, 142–143, 147–148, 157

individuals and **social systems**, 17, 20, 21, 22–23, 24, 107, 117–118, 148

industrial **capitalism**. *See* capitalism; industrial societies

Industrial Revolution, 58, 79–83, 100, 154

industrial societies, 98, 99, 100–101

inequality, 77–78, 83–85; conflict perspective on, 48–49, 53; crime and, 73–74; deviance and, 47; ecology and, 98–99; explanations of, 99–100; global, 77, 105–106; interaction and, 121, 122–124; population and, 105–106. *See also* capitalism; gender; oppression; poverty; privilege; race; social class; wealth, distribution of

inner cities, crisis in, 89–90. *See also* urbanization

innovative deviance, 73

interaction ritual, 120–121, 130. *See also* social interaction

Internet, 58–59, 94

iPod, production of, 21

Iraq, U.S. invasion of, 145

Ireland: historical status of women in, 78; racism and, 150; and subjugation by Great Britain, 150

Isla Vista, California, mass murder in, 10–11. *See also* mass murder

Italy, suicide rate in, 19

James, William, 10

Japan, concept of self in, 110

jazz improvisation as metaphor for social life, 118

jealousy, 75

Jefferson, Thomas, 151

Kaczynski, David, 43, 44

Kanter, Rosabeth Moss, 122–123

Katrina, Hurricane, 8

King, Martin Luther, Jr., 85–86

labor movement, 87; race and, 152

Langer, Susanne, 33–35, 60

language, 12, 32; gender and, 33–35; performative, 126–130; self and, 108–109

Last of the Mohicans, The, 144

Latinos/as, suicide among, 19

LGBT (lesbian, gay, bisexual, and transgender), 122, 122n

liberal solutions for poverty, 139–141

looking-glass self, 111

Losing Ground, 136–137

love, language and, 126–130

luxury of obliviousness, 155

manhood, patriarchal, 144–146. *See also* gender; men; patriarchy

Manifest Destiny, doctrine of, 152–153

Marx, Karl, 86–87, 98

Massacoe tribe, 154

mass media: concentration of control over, 55–56; violence and, 142

mass murder, 10–11, 142

material culture, 54–60

materialism, cultural, 95–96

Mead, George Herbert, 108–109, 111

Mead, Margaret, 81
means of production, ownership of, 86
men: death rates and, 103; and housework, 82, 88–89; teen pregnancy and, 141; violence and, 70–72, 141–146. *See also* family; gender; patriarchy; women
Merton, Robert K., 38, 72–74
Mexico: population growth in, 104–105; U.S. war with, 153
migration, population growth and, 100–101
mode of production, 98
Monopoly as social system, 14–15, 66
morality and cultural norms, 47
Mubarak, Hosni, 59
Murray, Charles, 136–140
music as culture, 54, 118
musical chairs as metaphor for capitalist economic system, 25, 135
Myrdal, Gunnar, 85–86
mythology, American, 144–146

Nantucket Island, Native Americans on, 49
Native Americans: conquest of, 144, 150, 152, 153, 154; cultures of, 49, 37–38; enslavement of, 151; suicide among, 19
nature, cultural beliefs about, 37–38
New Age thinking, 10
New Orleans, 8
Newtown, Connecticut, mass murder in, 142
niches, ecological, 98
nonindustrial societies, population in, 101
norms, cultural, 44–50; conflict perspective on, 48–50; functional perspective on, 46–48; of reciprocity, 128
Norway, culture of, compared with U.S. culture, 41
nuclear family, 88–89

Obama, Barack, 67; election of, 134; popularity of, 143
obvious truth as focus of sociology, 38–39
Occupy Wall Street movement, 57, 87, 140
one thing, the, 12
opportunity, distribution of, 72–74
oppression, 8. *See also* gender; heterosexism; inequality; patriarchy; privilege; race; social class

other, generalized, 111–112
other, significant, 111
overpopulation, 105–106

Parenti, Michael, 55–56
path of least resistance, 16–17; roles and, 68, 168n4; social change and, 155–156
patriarchal manhood. *See* manhood, patriarchal
patriarchy, 35, 77–78, 79–81, 99, 144–146. *See also* gender; men; women
performative language, 126–130
Perot, Ross, 132
personal solutions for social problems, 141. *See also* individualism
pollution, environmental, 25–26. *See also* ecology
population: energy use and, 105; growth of, 100–101; poverty and, 104–106; racial composition of, 101
post-industrial societies, 99
poverty: deviance and, 72–73; explanation of, 133–141. *See also* income; opportunity, distribution of; wealth, distribution of
power: concept of, 78; in families, 71–72, 79, 102; in schools, 85. *See also* power structure; social structure
power structure: and capitalism, 87, 140; coalitions and, 102; ecology and, 93; in families, 79, 102; and prejudice, 83; in schools, 85; social inequality and, 99, 131, 143, 153, 155, 156–157
prejudice, 50, 51, 83–85, 167n14. *See also* gender; heterosexism; oppression; patriarchy; privilege; race
presentation of self, 114–115
press, freedom of, 55–56
printing press as material culture, 55
privilege, 8–9, 18, 22–24, 40, 50–51, 77–78, 82, 99, 162–163, 167n14; interaction and, 123; tracing, 153–155
problems, social, 134
pronouns, **gender**, 34–35
property: capitalism and, 26, 87; idea of, 48–49
psychology: behavioral, 107; as way of thinking, 10, 19

queer, 122n

race: affirmative action and, 137, 152, 162–163; civil rights movement, 85–86; crime and, 94; death rates and, 103; idea of, 150, 152, 157; invention of, 149–151; in New Orleans, 8; segregation and, 22, 84–85, 94, 155–156; social class and, 136, 152, 155; suicide and, 19. *See also* privilege; racism; white privilege
racism, 13–14, 22–24, 83–85, 116–117. *See also* inequality; oppression; privilege; race; segregation, racial
reality, social construction of, 31–37, 38, 41, 60, 112, 118–121
rebels, conformity and, 113
reciprocity, norm of, 128
relationships, structure and, 64–65
religion, ecology and, 95–96
Republican Party, 132
ritual, interaction, 120–121, 130. *See also* social interaction
role conflict, 17, 68–69, 168n4
roles, 68; and the generalized other, 111–113; role conflict, 17, 68–69, 168n4; the self and, 110–112. *See also* dramaturgical perspective; role structure; social interaction; status
role structure, 75–76, 79–82, 88, 101–102. *See also* status
Romania, government control of typewriters in, 55
Room of One's Own, A, 93
Roosevelt, Theodore, 145

sabotage during the Industrial Revolution, 58
same-sex marriage, 85
Samoa, adolescence in, 81
San Miguel de Allende, Mexico, 63
schools: cheating in, 73–74; ecology of, 93; and families, 79–80; inequality and, 89–90; power structure in, 85; as social systems, 27–28; values in, 73–74
Schopenhauer, Arthur, 42
segregation, racial, 22, 84–85, 94, 155–156
self, 107–113; in systems, 113–118. *See also* individualism
sexual harassment, 68–70, 168n4. *See also* gender; patriarchy; sexual violence; violence
sexual orientation, 85. *See also* heterosexism; LGBT

sexual violence, 70–71. *See also* gender; patriarchy; violence
significant other, 111
silence about men's violence, 141–146
situational status, 67
Skinner, B. F., 107
slavery, 21, 70, 100, 151–152, 157
snakes, cultural attitudes about, 51–52
social class, 99; death rates and, 103; race and, 136, 152, 155; voting and, 131. *See also* capitalism; inequality; poverty
social construction of reality. *See* reality, social construction of
social identity, 110–112. *See also* self
social interaction, 113–121
socialization, 121–122
social problems, 24–27, 134–140
social status. *See* status.
social structure, 63–90; and culture, 83–88, 152; as distribution, 77–79; as relation 74–77. *See also* boundaries, community; distributions, structural; division of labor; family: power structures in; power structure; roles; status
social systems, 12, 27; analysis of social problems and, 24–27; corporations as, 13, 165n3; and ecosystems, 95; families as, 12, 70; individuals and, 107, 117, 148; in relation to other systems, 79–83, 88–90
society, 9, 11
sociology: defining, 3–5, 12; practice of, 1–3; as worldview, 147–149, 157
South Korea, capitalism in, 87
state, 87–88
status, 65–70; and the generalized other, 111–113; as relation, 74–75; and the self, 110–112, 163–164; types of, 67
stepparents, 76
stereotypes, 84–85
stigma, 47–48
strikebreakers, race and, 152
structural distributions. *See* distributions, structural
suburbs and inner cities, 89–90
suicide, 18–20, 103
Supreme Court, U.S., as social system, 66

sweatshops, 21
symbols, 33, 35–36. *See also* language

Tannen, Deborah, 121–122
technology: capitalism and, 58; and controlling the Internet, 59; and natural environment, 95, 97, 98
terrorism, 20–21
theater, social life as, 114–117
Thomas, Dorothy Swain, 38
Thomas, W. I., 38
Thoreau, Henry David, 153
time structure, 63–64

Unabomber, 43, 44
urbanization, 80, 89, 100
U.S. Congress, ecology of, 93–94
U.S. Constitution, race and, 151
U.S. Supreme Court as social system, 66

values, cultural, 39–44; conflict between, 43; deviance and, 72–74
Vietnam War, 145
violence: American mythology and, 144; domestic, 70–72; men's, invisibility of, 141–146; sexual, 70–71
voting, 131–134

waiting lines, social reality of, 120
Wampanoag tribe, 49
war: in Afghanistan, 145; explanation of, 20–21; in Iraq, 145; norms and, 45; Vietnam War, 145
wealth, distribution of, 49–50, 90, 139. *See also* capitalism; inequality; poverty; status
Weber, Max, 65n, 78
welfare reform: as solution to poverty, 136–137; voting and, 133
Wellman, David, 22
white privilege, origins of, 149–159
women: as artists and writers, 93; and death rates, 103; as deviant, 48; teenage pregnancy, 141. *See also* family; gender; men; patriarchy
Woolf, Virginia, 93
Woolworth's, racial segregation in, 155–156
worldview, 144n; changing, 157–159; sociology as, 147–149, 157

ALLAN G. JOHNSON is a nationally recognized sociologist, nonfiction author, novelist, and public speaker best known for his work on issues of privilege and oppression, especially in relation to gender and race. He is the author of numerous books, including *The Gender Knot: Unraveling Our Patriarchal Legacy* (Temple) and *Privilege, Power, and Difference*. His work has been translated into several languages and excerpted in numerous anthologies. Visit him online at www.agjohnson.us and follow his blog at www.agjohnson.wordpress.com.